Keys to the Kingdom

Impressioning, Privilege Escalation, Bumping, and Other Key-Based Attacks Against Physical Locks

Deviant Ollam
Shane Lawson, Technical Editor

ELSEVIER

AMSTERDAM • BOSTON • HEIDELBERG
LONDON • NEW YORK • OXFORD
PARIS • SAN DIEGO • SAN FRANCISCO
SINGAPORE • SYDNEY • TOKYO
Syngress is an imprint of Elsevier

Acquiring Editor: Chris Katsaropoulos
Development Editor: Heather Scherer
Project Manager: Paul Gottehrer
Designer: Alisa Andreola

Syngress is an imprint of Elsevier
225 Wyman Street, Waltham, MA 02451, USA

Notices

Knowledge and best practice in this field are constantly changing. As new research and experience broaden our understanding, changes in research methods or professional practices, may become necessary. Practitioners and researchers must always rely on their own experience and knowledge in evaluating and using any information or methods described herein. In using such information or methods they should be mindful of their own safety and the safety of others, including parties for whom they have a professional responsibility.

To the fullest extent of the law, neither the Publisher nor the authors, contributors, or editors, assume any liability for any injury and/or damage to persons or property as a matter of products liability, negligence or otherwise, or from any use or operation of any methods, products, instructions, or ideas contained in the material herein.

Library of Congress Cataloging-in-Publication Data
Application submitted

British Library Cataloguing-in-Publication Data
A catalogue record for this book is available from the British Library

ISBN: 978-1-59749-983-5

For information on all Syngress publications visit our
website at http://store.elsevier.com

Printed and bound by CPI Group (UK) Ltd, Croydon, CR0 4YY
Transferred to digital print 2012

Working together to grow
libraries in developing countries

www.elsevier.com | www.bookaid.org | www.sabre.org

ELSEVIER   BOOK AID
International   Sabre Foundation

Keys to the Kingdom

to Daisy

Do what you will, always.
Walk where you like, your steps.
Do as you please... I'll back you up.

Contents

Author's Note

This book was written over the course of six weeks, during which time I sat at my desk wearing my battered Navy watch cap alternately drinking bourbon and jasmine tea, as the same huge playlist repeated over and over and over again full of songs from Girlyman, Deadmau5, Gillian Welch, and the Ramones.

Without the love and support from my exceptional mother and father I would have never been in a position to do any of this wonderful exploration and research, nor would I have learned how to find words within myself to put upon these pages.

Thank you to Chris Katsaropoulos, Heather Sherer, Audrey Doyle, Paul Gottehrer, and everyone else at Syngress who was involved on this project. I always seem to choose very adventurous writing schedules and it's a miracle that we all can keep up with the deadlines. Special thanks to Shane Lawson for choosing to take on the role of Tech Editor a second time... he keeps me from looking too foolish and for that I am ever-grateful.

I must take a moment and offer my thanks and praise to all of the new TOOOL chapters which have been emerging across the United States and else-where. It's a remarkable inspiration to see all of this interest developing and to have so many new faces appear at TOOOL events. I could not possibly recognize and honor all of the people responsible, but I hope it will be sufficient to say that we all owe the new leadership of the chapters in Chicago, Detroit, Des Moines, Jacksonville, Kansas City, New York, Portland, Reno, Rochester, and Montréal a big hand. They, along with the old guard in places like Philadelphia, Princeton, Boston, Ann Arbor, Baltimore, and the San Francisco Bay Area, consistently help TOOOL to grow and reach more people and touch more lives.

TOOOL would like to thank all of the other sporting, hobbyist, and amateur lockpicking groups who help to spread knowledge and build interest in this fascinating field. SSDeV, LI, FALE, and the FOOLS are full of wonderful people who love to teach and have fun. An extra special thanks goes to Valanx, Dosman, and the rest of the FOOLS for reminding us to not be so serious, even when we have something serious to say.

Thank you to Barry Wels, Jos Weyers, Dennis van Zuijlekom, dosman, datagram, and Patrick Thomas for your terrific photos and friendship.

I must thank my roommates Babak Javadi and Andrew Righter for their support and understanding during this and all of my other projects. They are incredibly considerate whenever I must sequester myself in my office for 18-hour days without joining in to cook house dinners and they are always supportive of my busy travel schedule, showing a willingness to feed and look after my cats while I am away. (They have also shown unbelievably tolerance when these felines act up or pee on something that they shouldn't!)

Thank you to Dark Tangent for first suggesting that I turn my lockpicking content into training course, and to Ping Look and everyone else who works tirelessly so that Black Hat can keep ticking along.

Extra special thanks to Bruce and Heidi for ShmooCon, where I gave my very first public lecture about lockpicking. You and all those who put in the monumental effort every year are the reason ShmooCon remains my favorite conference to this day.

I also must give a terrific shout-out to the organizers of other conferences, large and small, who have graciously allowed my associates and I to descend upon your event with all of our bulky hardware in order to set up Lockpick Villages where attendees can learn and play. We must offer our thanks to…

- The amazing DEFCON Goons and support staff who show up in Vegas every summer
- The whole 2600 crew behind the HOPE conferences
- Nickerson, Jack Daniel, and the whole BSides team
- SkyDog, Robin, and their clan who bring us Outerzone and the Otherzone
- Andrzej Targosz, Anna Kołodziejczyk, Sławomir Jabs, Emilia Staszczak, Jakub Kozio, Pavol Luptak, and all of the ProIdea folks who put CONFidence together and give us license to create amazing new games there
- David and Erin Kennedy, IronGeek, and PureHate for exploding on to the scene with DerbyCon
- Jason Martin and the SecureDNA team at ShakaCon… we're so glad to be seeing you again soon!
- David, Tim, and the whole ToorCon crew, we look forward to camping this summer.
- Ton Slewe, Elly van den Heuvel, and Everyone at the NCSC who puts on GovCERT. Extra thanks to Marnix who is unbelievably hospitable whenever I am in Amsterdam

… we also want to send our best regards to everyone behind events like QuarterCon, ReCon, GrrCON, QuahogCon, RootFest, hackademic, SeaCure.IT, NotACon, SummerCon, You sh0t the Sherrif, and more. We don't always make it to every single one of your events and some of you are still establishing yourselves, but we always value times when we can visit and bring some fun lockpicking content for your attendees.

An extra special thanks must go to Christina Pei for coordinating with Dale, Kate, and everyone else at Maker Faire. TOOOL has been reaching out to so many new groups of people, including families big and small, due to our exposure at Maker events. We hope that this trend continues and we always look forward to teaching the next generation of lockpickers.

This work would not have been possible had I not met Babak Javadi, who has given endless advice, encouragement, and invaluable constructive criticism of my material.

I owe such gratitude to the close friends and loved ones who kept me from losing my mind while writing this book. Nancy, you kept my stress level from red-lining when I was ready to blow a gasket more than one time. Beckie, you surprised me with unexpected smiles that picked me up when I was low. Kim, I can always count on you to talk. Roni, I can always count on you to listen. Ty, Natc, Doris, and JJ... your music reaches me in a way that little else can when I am at my wit's end. Keep on writing, keep on performing, take care of little Jango, and come around soon to see us all again.

Perhaps the most special thank-you of all in this book should go to Stephanie... at a time when I felt particularly lost and adrift, you were kind to me and reminded me of many wonderful things that I hadn't been able to see for quite a while. The softness of your words and the steadfast support you have shown me in recent months is beyond anything imaginable. This book may not have been completed on time had it not been for your encouragement and understanding.

It is with considerable sadness that I had to embark upon this project without Daisy Belle at my side. I cannot deny that the finished work suffered because of your absence. I miss you every day, and part of me still writes and speaks and tries to achieve simply because I want to make you proud of me. I will always love you.

... and, as always, a special thank-you to those in the hacker community who *get involved*. Those who attend conferences, prepare presentations, research exploits and publicly disclose them properly, those who continue seeking new skills, who want to explore, who want to understand, who want to learn, touch, and do. To anyone who has ever sat in one of my lectures and asked an insightful question or gone home to try out what they have learned... to anyone who has not just watched but gotten up and tried their hand at Gringo Warrior, Pandora's Lock Box, the Defiant Box, ClusterPick, Locksport Wizard, or any of the other contests that I have run over the years... to all those who make the community what it is... I thank you from the bottom of my heart.

About the Author

Deviant Ollam's first and strongest love has always been teaching. A graduate of the New Jersey Institute of Technology's Science, Technology, and Society program, he is always fascinated by the interplay that connects human values and social trends to developments in the technical world. While earning his BS degree at NJIT, Deviant also completed the History degree program federated between that institution and Rutgers University.

While paying the bills as a security auditor and penetration testing consultant with The CORE Group, Deviant is also a member of the Board of Directors of the U.S. division of TOOOL, The Open Organisation Of Lockpickers. Every year at DEFCON and ShmooCon Deviant runs the Lockpicking Village, and he has conducted physical security training sessions for Black Hat, DeepSec, ToorCon, HackCon, ShakaCon, HackInTheBox, ekoparty, AusCERT, GovCERT, CONFidence, the FBI, the NSA, DARPA, and the United States Military Academy at West Point. His favorite Amendments to the U.S. Constitution are, in no particular order, the 1st, 2nd, 9th, and 10th.

About the Technical Editor

Shane Lawson is the Director of Commercial and Federal Security Solutions in the Cyber Security Division of Tenacity Solutions, Inc. where he focuses on penetration testing, security assessments, and supply chain risk analysis for his clients. He previously served as a senior technical adviser and security analyst for numerous federal agencies and private sector firms. In his free time, Shane researches physical security systems and teaches others about physical security bypass mechanisms. Shane is a U.S. Navy veteran, where he served as an information systems security manager and communications watch officer for over 10 years.

Impressioning

CHAPTER OUTLINE

A topic that has generated great interest and discussion among lock pickers and penetration testers in recent years is the tactic of impressioning. Of course, like many exciting trends that capture the attention of the security industry, impressioning is not brand new. As is the case with most lock-opening methods, this has been a skill in the arsenal of locksmiths and covert operatives for some time... however, precious little has been written or reported about it publicly. Only in recent years has the topic of impressioning received increased focus at security conferences and locksport competitions.

As you will soon see, there is legitimate reason to be excited about impressioning. Not only is the tactic *very* covert—at least outwardly—but if it is completed properly, you will have essentially compromised your target lock for good. A successful lock picking attack means you have opened the lock in that particular instance. A successful impressioning attack means that you have opened the lock in perpetuity.

THE MECHANICS OF PIN TUMBLER LOCKS

Although many of you are likely already familiar with the means by which mechanical locks function, it would be appropriate to give a brief overview of such facts here, to ensure that all readers are comfortable with this concept and to introduce the style of diagrams that I like to use in all of my instructional materials which pertain to locks.

The style of lock with which the majority of people are most acquainted is the pin tumbler design. I realize that many of you may already be familiar with this hardware (indeed, diagrams and photographs of all shapes and sizes abound on the Internet and in other printed works), but I feel it would be proper to review this mechanism briefly, in order to guarantee that all readers understand how it functions and how it can be exploited.

The pin tumbler mechanism is one of the oldest lock designs in existence and is still widely used today. It consists of a round component referred to as a *plug* which rotates in order to engage or move some additional mechanism (such as a latch or cam or tailpiece connected to the rear side of the plug). When the lock is at rest, the plug is blocked from rotating by means of pins. These pins are installed in such a way as to prevent turning of the plug. Only if the pins are moved to a precise position (usually by inserting the correct key into the lock) can the plug become unobstructed and free to move.

The basic diagram that I like to use in all of my instruction about locks can be seen in Figure 1.1. This is an image of a pin tumbler lock, seen from both a forward-facing perspective (on the left side of this diagram) and from a side-view perspective (on the right side of this diagram). In this image, the *plug* referred to above is shown in a rather bright shade of yellow. The plug is situated in the *housing,* which in my diagrams is shown in a pale beige hue. The pins which prevent (or allow) the plug to turn appear in two varieties: key pins (shown in red) and driver pins (shown in blue) and they are acted upon by

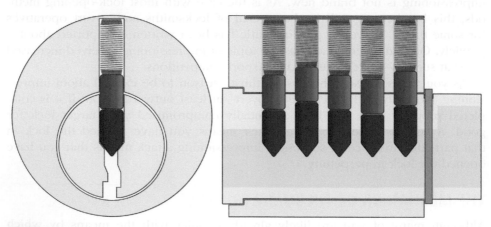

FIGURE 1.1

Here we see all the basic components of a pin tumbler lock. The plug, the housing, the pins, and the springs… most of the locks which we use every day consist of little more than these simple pieces.

springs installed in each pin chamber. As you can see in Figure 1.1, when the lock is at rest it is the driver pins which obstruct the plug's movement.

Pin tumbler lock operation

When a user inserts the proper key into a lock, the key pins ride along the edge of the key's blade (see Figure 1.2). The blade travels into the lock until the key comes to rest either by its tip encountering the rear of the keyway or by the key's shoulder coming to rest on the front face of the lock. Locks that function in this manner are called *tip-stopped* or *shoulder-stopped,* respectively.

When the proper key has been fully inserted into a lock, a unique phenomenon can be observed... all of the pin stacks will have been pushed into exactly the right position such that the split between the key pins and driver pins (known as the pin shear line) will be aligned across the edge of the plug. When the pin stacks are all in this perfect position, there is nothing obstructing the plug from turning. This alignment is represented in Figure 1.3.

Let's take a closer look at this phenomenon, without the appearance of a key in our diagrams, to ensure that everyone is fully-aware of what is taking place. Figure 1.4 shows quite clearly how all the pin stacks have now been raised to a height that will allow the plug to move freely and rotate within the housing. The key pins (shown in red) are all contained perfectly within the plug, and the driver pins (shown in blue) have all been moved completely out of the plug and are resting in the housing. If a user were attempting to operate this lock, it would turn feely, as seen in Figure 1.5.

For a lock to operate and for the plug to turn, all pin stacks must be in the appropriate position. A key with an incorrect size in even one position will fail

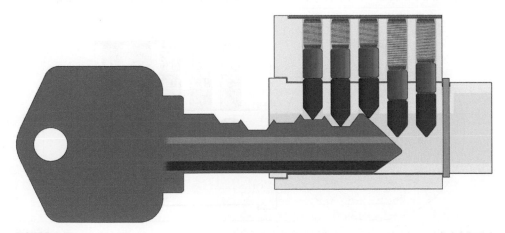

FIGURE 1.2
A key being inserted into a pin tumbler lock. Its blade moves the pin stacks as it rides against them.

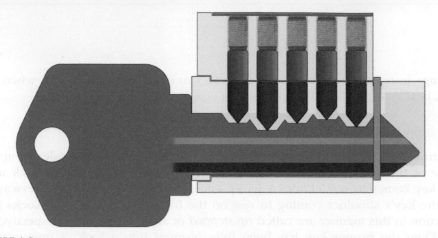

FIGURE 1.3
The correct key for this lock has been fully inserted.

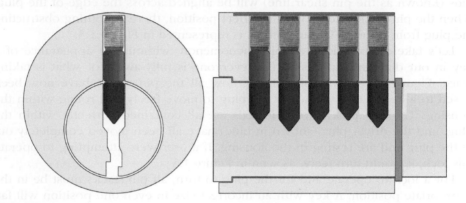

FIGURE 1.4
At this point, the plug is free to rotate within the housing because no pin stacks are binding.

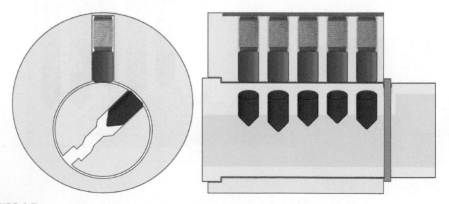

FIGURE 1.5
The plug of the lock can be seen rotated.

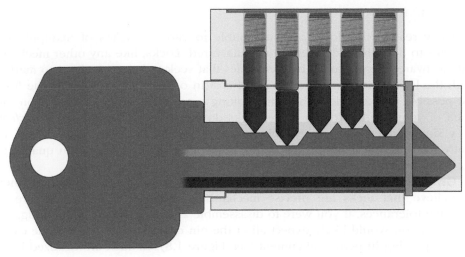

FIGURE 1.6

In this diagram, one cut on the blade of the key is too deep, and the resulting misalignment of the pin stack in that position will cause a driver pin (seen in blue) to prevent the plug from turning.

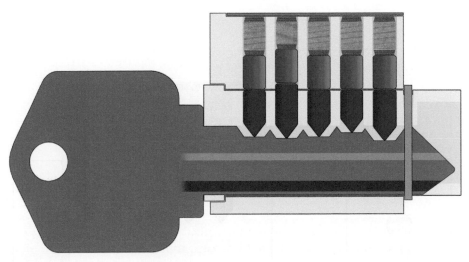

FIGURE 1.7

In this diagram, one cut on the blade of the key is too shallow, and the resulting misalignment of the pin stack in that position will cause a key pin (seen in red) to prevent the plug from turning.

to operate the lock. As can be seen in the following images, if a single position on a key is cut too deeply (Figure 1.6) or too shallow (Figure 1.7) then this will not result in a perfect alignment of pins when the key is inserted and the plug will be unable to rotate easily because one pin stack will still be binding.

Pin tumbler lock imperfections

The key reason that locks are susceptible to various means of manipulation pertains to how these devices are manufactured. Locks, like any other mechanical hardware, are produced by companies that seek to bring products to market with the least amount of overhead and cost in order to retail them at the lowest possible market price while still making a profit. In order to appear on the shelf of your local hardware store, locks do not need to be absolutely *perfect,* they simply need to work reliably and repeatedly under most conditions. In truth, most people have an inaccurate perception of the production quality of the locks that they use every day.

Given what you have seen in the previous diagrams, you might be inclined to believe that locks are precise mechanisms, produced with great care to exacting tolerances. If you were to disassemble a lock and observe the plug, for example, you would likely expect all of the pin chambers to be the same exact size, appearing in perfect alignment (see Figure 1.8). In such an idealized lock, all of the pin stacks would likewise be perfectly aligned. If someone were to attempt to rotate the plug without any key present, all of the driver pins would be subject to a binding force... they would all equally and simultaneously prevent the plug from rotating (see Figure 1.9).

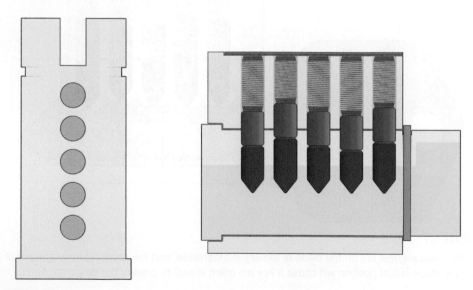

FIGURE 1.8

A "perfect" lock. The left side of the diagram shows the lock's plug as viewed from above. In this idealized hypothetical scenario, all of the pin chambers are drilled in perfect alignment.

In the real world, however, the process of manufacturing locks is rife with possibilities for error and imperfection. Mechanical tolerances are not absolute, and factors such as machine wear, imperfect raw materials, and imprecise quality control result in the production of locks where not all of the component parts are perfectly aligned. Figure 1.10 is a much more accurate representation of locks as they are found in the real world.

The photographs in Figures 1.11 and 1.12 show pieces of a brand new lock which was disassembled directly out of the box. The imperfections seen on the plug and the pins are not the result of wear and tear from time in the field, but rather they are representative of the condition in which many locks are shipped straight from their manufacturer.

When a "real world" lock is subjected to turning force (in the absence of the correct key) it does *not* behave in the manner shown in Figure 1.9. Instead, the various misalignments cause the pin stacks to bind with uneven pressure. In almost all situations, these mechanical imperfections will result in one pin stack binding more than any other (see Figures 1.13 and 1.14). It is this uneven binding within locks that makes it possible to attack them in all manner of ways.

Because locks tend to *bind* one pin at a time when the plug is subjected to turning force, it is often possible to *attack* locks one pin at a time. This is the case with the tactic of lock picking, as was seen in my previous book. It is also the case with impressioning, which is the focus of this chapter.

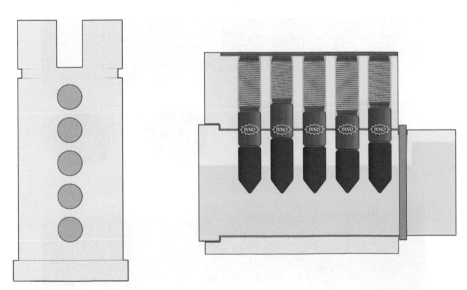

FIGURE 1.9

If turning force is applied to the plug of this "perfect" lock without any key present, all of the driver pins will "bind" simultaneously, preventing the plug from rotating.

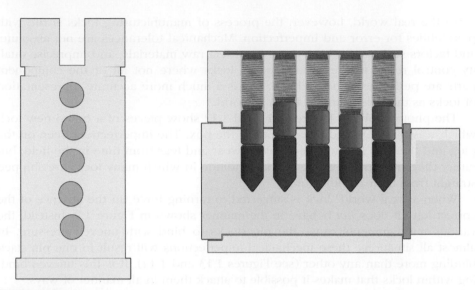

FIGURE 1.10

A lock as found in the "real world"... this image may appear quite similar to the one in Figure 1.8, but pay close attention to the left side of the diagram where the plug is represented. Do you see the misalignment and imperfection of the pin chambers when you view the plug from above?

FIGURE 1.11

The plug of a typical mass-produced lock. Note the misalignment and poor tolerances seen in the drilling of the pin chambers. *(Photo by Austin Appel)*

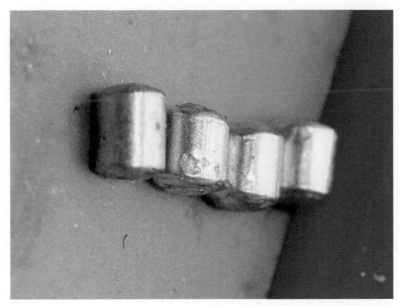

FIGURE 1.12

Pins from a typical mass-produced lock. Note the blemishes and imperfections that are a byproduct of the manufacturing process. *(Photo by Austin Appel)*

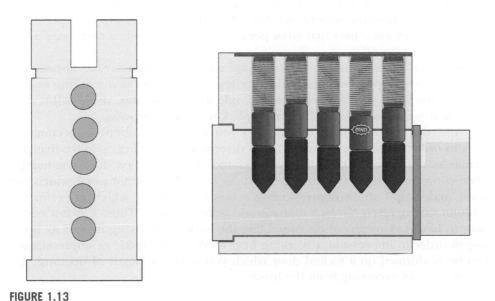

FIGURE 1.13

In the real world, a lock whose plug is subjected to turning force will tend to experience "binding" on one pin stack more than any other.

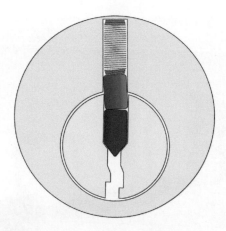

FIGURE 1.14

This front view of a lock shows how a pin stack will "bind" if it is not moved out of the way when turning force is applied to the plug.

WHAT IS IMPRESSIONING?

In a single sentence, impressioning can be described as "turning a blank key into a working key in order to open a lock." However, such a simple definition omits some rather critical elements of this process, and describing this attack in those words alone will usually result in quizzical looks from some people or expressions of non-amazement in others. More than once I have seen people in training classes ask, "Isn't that what people do every day when they copy a key at a hardware store?"

Thus, we come to the first of two important points concerning impressioning... this whole process is performed *without any access to a working key for the lock you are trying to open.* Once people understand this, they realize right away that we're not talking about a simple key-copying process.

"Ah," the doubters then remark, "so you are talking about inspecting the pins in order to measure them and thus determine the bitting code for that particular lock... which would allow you to hand-file a key or produce one using a code-cutting machine." This brings us to the second important point which you must understand about impressioning... this is an attack which is performed *without taking apart the lock that you are trying to open.* Thus, it is not necessary to have any means of disassembling the lock or removing it from its housing in order to impression a working key. In short, the tactic of impressioning can be performed on a locked door which you have no means of opening, disassembling, or accessing from the inside.

All that is needed to impression a key for a lock is a blank that will fit in the keyway. Most of the time, this is a trivial consideration. Most locks do not have what are known as "restricted profiles" or "restricted keyways", which are means of controlling the market supply of blank keys for a particular brand or model. Even for locks that *are* restricted in some way, it is often possible to acquire blank keys either through back channels within the locksmithing industry or by producing them yourself on specialized hardware such as an Easy Entrie key-producing machine (see Figure 1.15).

FIGURE 1.15

An Easy Entrie machine is a specialized device used to mill down the sides of special billets of brass in order to effectively produce blank keys for any lock, including locks with restricted keyways. The Easy Entrie machine in this photo is owned by the U.S. division of The Open Organisation Of Lockpickers.

> **NOTE**
>
> One interesting point about impressioning is how much opinion varies—even among lockpickers and locksmiths—concerning the most appropriate way to use this term. Some people will use the phrase "key impressioning" while others claim that this is incorrect and insist that people should call it "lock impressioning" instead. Jos Weyers, an inernationally-recognized champion competitor in this field for many years running, typically calls it "key impressioning" but acknowledges that he also routinely uses the phrase "to impression a lock" (although he admits that "lock impressioning" seems to hit his ear in an unpleasant way).
>
> Personally, I tend to believe that this is a situation where it takes two to tango… you can't "impression a lock" without a key and you can't "impression a key" in the absence of a lock. So, then, is the best terminology one that incorporates both pieces of hardware? Clearly, "lock and key impressioning" is far too long and clumsy a phrase to be used with regularity. (And, even then, I'm certain that there would be arguments as to *which* bit of hardware should be mentioned first!)
>
> In this book, the word "impressioning" will often stand alone. On one hand, this is my attempt to side-step the criticism of those who are perhaps a bit too passionate about their preferred nomenclature; on the other, this is my way of tacitly acknowledging that neither implement is more important than the other when you are attempting this attack.

It is quite simple

As you will see in the following sections of this chapter, nothing is needed in the way of expensive equipment or complex machinery when you are impressioning. No power tools or code-cutting key machines are used. No digital calipers or advanced measuring devices are required. The entire attack can be (and almost always is) performed completely manually, without anything that operates using electricity (save for the occasional bit of illumination from a lamp.)

At its most basic, to impression a lock only a few specific things are needed…

- A blank key that fits into the lock (Frankly, having more than one key is generally a good idea, as it is quite common to break keys during attempts at impressioning.)
- A means of solidly gripping your blank key (Hardware store tools like Vice-Grips can be used, but having a "proper" impressioning handle makes a big difference.)
- A hand file for making cuts on the key blade (We will speak a great deal about types of files needed in the upcoming "Tips and Tricks" section of this chapter.)
- A source of magnification (While this isn't an absolute necessity from a mechanical standpoint, having proper magnification—and, along with it, proper *illumination*—will make all the difference in the world when you are impressioning a key.)
- Time (Impressioning will often take longer than lockpicking, but it will also tend to be more covert provided proper caution is taken and will yield greater returns in the long run, as you will see in the next section.)

WHY CHOOSE IMPRESSIONING?

When first hearing about impressioning, many people will ask when they would ever opt to attack a lock using a tactic that takes longer and is more tedious than lockpicking. "If I can pick a lock in approximately five minutes," a student once asked me, "what would be the benefit of an attack that might take as long as a half hour?"

This is a perfectly legitimate question. Indeed, many times lockpicking is an adequate—or even superior—means of entry to a secured area. However, if we compare these two tactics in greater detail, it should become clear that certain situations call for a degree of discretion and repeatability that can only be achieved by impressioning. The following hypothetical examples should illustrate the benefits of impressioning in greater detail.

The watchful eye

Consider a door to a secured area. This could be an outer door to a building, a door to a server room inside a company, or simply an executive lounge with restricted membership. In each of these examples, it is entirely possible that activity near these doors may be monitored in some way. Perhaps a security guard routinely walks around the perimeter of the building. Maybe there is a security camera that is trained on the server room's entrance. The executive lounge might have people entering and exiting at unpredictable times.

In all three of these examples, it could prove quite difficult to find the time to squat by these doors and use picking tools in order to open the lock. Even with an additional person serving as a lookout, dealing with concerns like a security patrol or the slow panning of a security camera or the comings and goings of people who are authorized to use a door which you are trying to compromise is not a recipe for easy execution of an attack like lockpicking. In the event that you have to hide or otherwise leave the area, this will effectively negate any progress that you have made. After all, there is really no way to leave a lock "half-picked" and return to finish opening it later. (Technically, I suppose, you could leave a tension tool in the lock with a small weight hanging from its handle... but this is by no means covert!)

The simple fact is that *picking* open a lock is an attack that must happen all at once. If you have to remove your tools and leave the lock for any reason, all of the pins will reset and you will be forced to start over anew when you return... often with little knowledge that will help you on this subsequent attempt (save for perhaps some sense of the order in which certain pins were binding during a previous effort). You will soon learn how impressioning is an attack that can be distributed over time... you can approach a lock, work on it briefly, then walk away completely (typically leaving the lock unchanged and without any outward indications of attack), and you will be free to resume your efforts in the future right where you left off, without losing any ground.

Also, the time spent *directly in front of the lock itself* can often be very minimal when you are impressioning a key. Five to ten *seconds* is all it usually takes to insert a key, move it slightly, and then pull it back out and walk away. This is easily something that can be done while avoiding security patrols. You could even time it so as to avoid the slow, regular sweep of a moving camera. Attacking a door where people are routinely entering and exiting? That's not a problem, either... simply approach like any other user (perhaps while on your phone or otherwise pretending to be distracted) and insert your "key," only to "realize that you have forgotten something" and pretend that you have to walk away moments later, before actually "unlocking" the door. Passers-by will almost always be none the wiser to your tactics.

Day and night

Imagine a different situation... one in which the door to a confidential-documents room in a highly secured facility is kept locked 100% of the time, and which is also wired with an entry sensor connected to an alarm circuit. During the daytime, when the building is full of people working, perhaps the door is not monitored. The numerous entry and exit events might be logged, but they do not result in an alarm going off. After 5:00 P.M., however, the office becomes empty and this hypothetical door is then no longer used... and opening it will result in an alert and a security response.

Lockpicking would not be an ideal means of entry in this scenario. Not only does it require conspicuous tools (tools that might even be detected and confiscated by guards at the building's entrance, depending on just how "secure" the facility is designed to be), but the act of squatting by a door during business hours in an occupied building is hardly something I would normally care to attempt. However, because of the alarm system and the door entry sensor, it would not be feasible to sneak in and pick the lock on the door after-hours... even if you were successful, what then? Would you wait there until morning, keeping your hand on the tension tool the whole time, hoping to somehow enter the secure room at the stroke of 9:00 A.M. when the alarm settings are relaxed? Impressioning would be an ideal attack to use in a situation like this.

If I were running a penetration test against a building such as this, I would instruct operatives to enter the facility during normal business hours, carrying only blank keys and something to serve as an impressioning handle. All of these items would look innocuous. I would have these operatives wait until after 5:00 P.M., then make a brief attempt to begin the impressioning process... approaching the door, inserting a key for a second, then exiting the building and appearing to simply be someone who was finishing a phone call or otherwise working a little late. Then, safely away from this whole facility the key could be inspected, adjusted slightly, and the same process could be repeated on another day... possibly by an entirely *different* operative. After some time, when a functional key had been finally created, someone would be able to enter the facility during business hours, approach the secure door quite normally, and enter without difficulty or incident… and without setting off any alarms. Results like this could never happen with lockpicking alone.

Quite nice, but can you do it twice?

The final hypothetical scenario that can demonstrate the extreme usefulness of impressioning is one that many penetration specialists can appreciate. Imagine a locked wiring closet containing communication hardware such as routers, switches, perhaps even a telephone PBX control box. Let's say you want to insert a specialist into this room, someone who is highly-trained in Cisco systems, teleco equipment, and signal interception. This person may lack any training in physical security matters. Using lockpicking to allow this technician into the wiring closet could require an additional operative who would have to accompany the first specialist in order to manipulate the lock… if you were trying to be *very* surreptitious, that second person might possibly even have to stick around the whole time, in order to re-lock the door once the job was complete. This would make the whole affair far less covert, since two people will often stand out far more than one lone individual.

If you were to opt for an impressioning attack, however, it is possible to be far more clandestine. The physical security specialist on your team could attack the lock (possibly in a very methodical and distributed manner, as described in the previous scenarios), and then simply *give the working key to the other technician,* who would be able to enter and exit the room with ease, entirely by himself.

Therein we see the usefulness of impressioning. It can be distributed over time, looks rather innocuous while being performed, and is a "one and done" solution if performed successfully. The next section of this chapter will demonstrate exactly how it works.

HOW IMPRESSIONING WORKS

The following description of the impressioning process is based around the same pin tumbler lock that was first shown in Figure 1.1. Imagine a blank key inserted in this lock, as seen in Figure 1.16. All of the pin stacks would be pushed "up" (in the context of this diagram) such that the driver pins would be entirely out of the plug, and in all of the chambers it would then be the key pins preventing the plug from turning.

> **NOTE**
>
> Readers of my first book may recall that I have a distaste for region-specific terms such as "top pin" or "bottom pin" given that one person's notion of which direction in a lock would be referred to as "up" might vary depending on where they live. Locks in much of Europe are mounted in a way that appears almost "upside down" to many North American observers. I hope to use neutral terminology whenever possible in this book, as well.

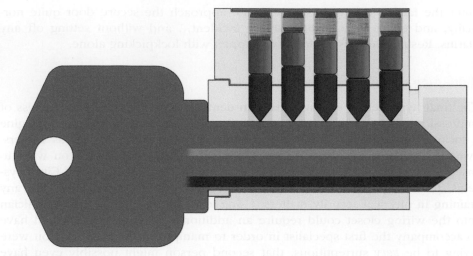

FIGURE 1.16

A blank key inserted into a lock. This will push all of the driver pins completely out of the plug and move the key pins into positions that will then prevent the plug from turning.

If an attempt is made to turn this blank key in its current position within the lock, naturally it will not work. The *driver* pins (having been pushed out of the plug) are not binding, as the case would be when you tension a lock with *no* key present, but the *key* pins are in the way. However, recall what was discussed earlier in this chapter and in other materials you may have read about attacking locks. Remember that due to manufacturing imperfections, pins within a lock rarely, if ever, bind equally when pressure is applied.

If an attempt is made to turn the plug of a lock when a blank key has been inserted, one pin stack will bind considerably more than the others (see Figure 1.17).

Now, with a blank key inserted and turned to one direction, the moment is right for the real work of impressioning… producing marks on the blade of the key. It is a somewhat difficult concept to understand at first, but what one must do at this time is attempt to "wiggle" the key in an up-and-down manner. I realize that this sounds like an impossible task. After all, most keys are not purely flat pieces of metal, but rather they are contoured with ridges and valleys. These features correspond to the unique shape of the keyway profile in the lock (known as the warding) and this leaves very limited means for the key itself to move *vertically* in the lock when it is inserted. After all, that is one of the primary functions of the profile warding… to seat and align the key so that it does not drift out of alignment during use.

However, all mechanical systems have at least a small degree of space between their components. There must be some allowance for manufacturing imperfections as well as wear and tear over time. Although a key cannot be

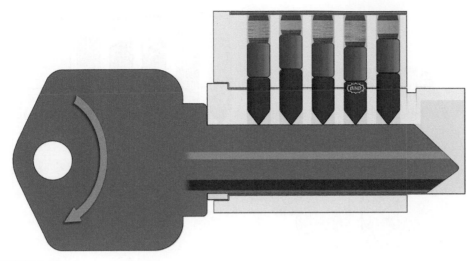

FIGURE 1.17

When the blank key in this example is forced in a clockwise direction, one pin stack (in this case, pin stack #4) will bind more than any of the others.

forced *a considerable distance* up or down within the keyway, it can be moved *a minuscule amount* if effort is applied... and this minuscule amount is all that is needed to perform the act of impressioning.

With the key in the lock, and with considerable "turning" pressure being maintained, one attempts to move the key upward and downward. Figure 1.18 represents what happens when this is attempted. Most of the pins in the lock are not binding at this time; they are free to move up and down within their respective chambers. All of these non-binding pins will simply jiggle slightly, but ultimately they will have no influence on any other piece of hardware.

The stack where the key pin is binding, however, is another story altogether. Since this pin stack is binding, it will not be so easy to move it vertically. When the key is jiggled up and down, the binding pin stack will resist this movement and the tip of the key pin will rub against the blade of the key, leaving a small mark. If you remove the key from the lock and inspect it, this mark will be visible (it may, however, be considerably difficult to see without the aid of magnification or additional illumination). Figure 1.19 shows a key that has been marked by the act of turning and wiggling. Figure 1.20 features the same key with an arrow pointing to this very small mark.

> **NOTE**
>
> If the mark on the blade of the key shown in these diagrams is difficult to see, you must forgive me. Something I am trying to convey with these images is just how small and hard to identify these marks will often be. Photographs of real keys will be shown later in this chapter and I hope they will further clarify just how difficult it sometimes can be to locate impressioning marks during this process.

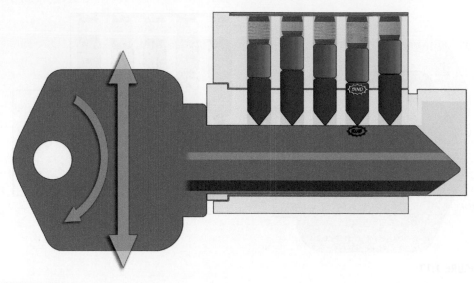

FIGURE 1.18

When the key is jiggled up and down, the binding pin stack will resist this movement and the tip of the key pin will rub against the blade of the key, leaving a small mark.

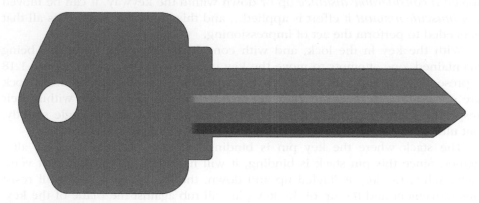

FIGURE 1.19

A key that has been subjected to turning and wiggling should bear a small mark where one pin stack was binding.

One interesting thing about mechanical tolerances and variations within locks is that seldom are they symmetrical. That is to say, an attempt to turn a lock in one direction may bind a particular pin stack… but then a subsequent attempt to turn the plug in the opposite direction will tend to cause an entirely different pin stack to bind. This is useful during impressioning, because it allows us to mark the key in multiple places at once, saving a good deal of time.

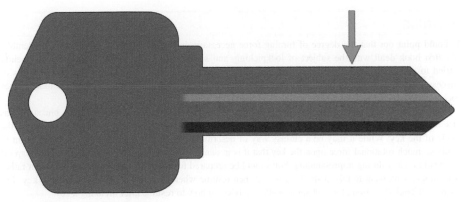

FIGURE 1.20

A key that has been subjected to turning and wiggling should bear a small mark where one pin stack was binding. The green arrow points to the small mark on the key's blade, which is quite difficult to see.

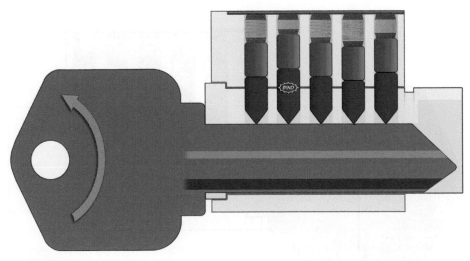

FIGURE 1.21

Turning the key in the opposite direction as before (in this case, turning the key counter-clockwise) should cause an entirely different pin stack to bind. In the hypothetical example shown in this diagram, it is now pin stack #2 that is binding.

Consider the key that had just been marked by turning in a clockwise direction and wiggling up and down. If that same key were inserted in the lock and turned in a counter-clockwise direction, a different pin stack would most likely bind (see Figure 1.21).

WARNING

I should point out that the degree of turning force necessary during impressioning is quite considerable. My first book dealt with the subject of lockpicking, and some of my readers may recall how frequently I tried to emphasize that lockpicking is a delicate art, where subtlety and finesse are the watchwords of success. Too much turning pressure (for instance, too much force used upon a tension tool) makes lockpicking very difficult.

This is NOT the case with impressioning. During impressioning, you want to bind pin stacks as absolutely tightly and firmly as you possibly can, so that they may make more pronounced marks on the blade of the key. While it may be a clumsy way of describing this, I will say that you essentially want to apply so much rotational force upon the key that it is in danger of breaking. Indeed, it is *typical* to snap off the head of a key during impressioning. You should be prepared for this; it is not a sign of failure, but rather it is simply a moment to take a short break and then resume where you left off by using another key. The "Tips and Tricks" section of this chapter contains advice on how to resume after breaking a key.

If upward and downward jiggling is attempted with the key turned in this new direction, an impressioning mark should be left on the blade in a different location than the one seen before (see Figures 1.22, 1.23, 1.24, and 1.25).

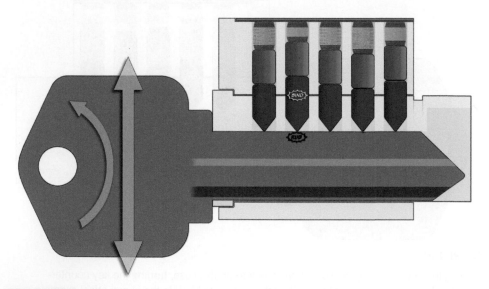

FIGURE 1.22

With counter-clockwise turning pressure being maintained, an attempt is made to jiggle the key in an up-and-down manner. This will cause the pin stack that is binding (in this case, pin #2) to rub against the blade of the key, hopefully leaving a mark.

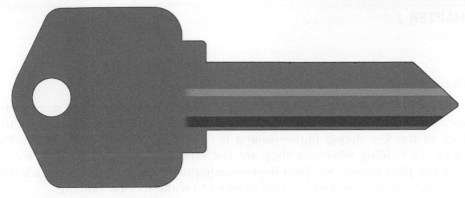

FIGURE 1.23

A key after it has been turned and wiggled in both clockwise and counter-clockwise directions. There are two distinct impressioning marks present.

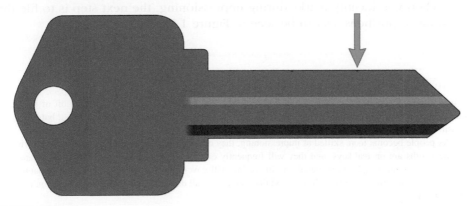

FIGURE 1.24

An arrow points to the mark left from the clockwise rotation and wiggling, when key pin #4 was binding.

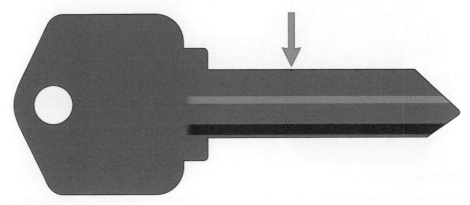

FIGURE 1.25

An arrow points to the mark left from the counter-clockwise rotation and wiggling, when key pin #2 was binding.

What do these marks indicate?

Now that we have these marks, you may be asking what the next step in the process is. Well, consider what these marks represent. Each mark seen on the blade of the key during impressioning is caused by a binding pin stack. Pin stacks are binding whenever they are not raised to the height which would allow the plug to turn. So, each impressioning mark represents a pin stack that would have to be raised or lowered in order to make it cease binding.

Since the process was started with a blank key, there is no conceivable way that these pin stacks should be any "higher" than they are right now. Thus, pin stacks in locations where small impressioning marks were spotted must be "lowered" in order to move them into their ideal position and allow the plug to turn. When you identify marks during impressioning, the next step is to file the key in those positions, as can be seen in Figure 1.26.

WARNING

When you are just starting out with impressioning, take care to not file too much material off of the key during each pass. Remember, it is always possible to re-examine marks and file further down… but it is *not* possible to take brass shavings and put them back onto the blade of the key if you have gone too far.

As people become more skilled at impressioning, they often start to learn just how specific the various bitting depths are on real keys, and they will frequently employ assorted measuring tools as a means of filing their cuts to manufacturer-specific positions. We will cover this sort of tactic later in this chapter… but for now, know that subtlety is the rule and that gradual, small degrees of filing are best when you're just starting out.

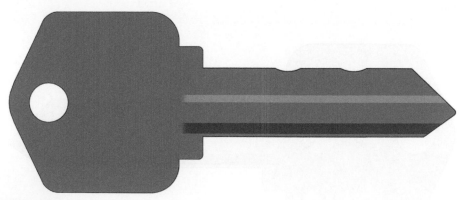

FIGURE 1.26

This key has now been filed down slightly in the two positions where marks were seen. It has only been filed a very small amount, since we would not want to over-shoot and cut too deeply into the blade. If greater depth is required, we will know because the pins should continue to mark in the same manner that they did before.

Once the key has been filed slightly in these two positions, the process continues. The key is inserted into the lock again. Figure 1.27 shows that very little has changed in the lock at this time. None of the pin stacks are in a considerably different position than they had been previously.

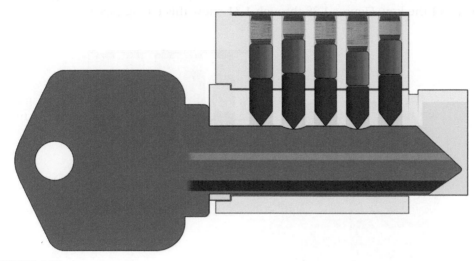

FIGURE 1.27

After filing, the key is re-inserted into the lock. The pin stacks in positions 2 and 4 have moved "down" slightly, but not much else has changed.

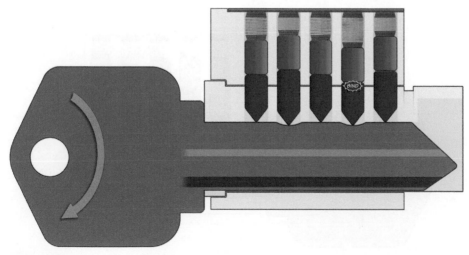

FIGURE 1.28

Clockwise pressure on the key causes pin stack #4 to bind, just as it did before.

If the same process as before is repeated—with considerable turning pressure being applied on one direction and the key is wiggled up and down, followed by considerable turning pressure in the opposite direction and more wiggling—then similar results as before should be expected. Pin stacks that are made to bind should resist the up-and-down movement and specific pins will rub against the blade of the key. Figures 1.28 through 1.31 show this taking place.

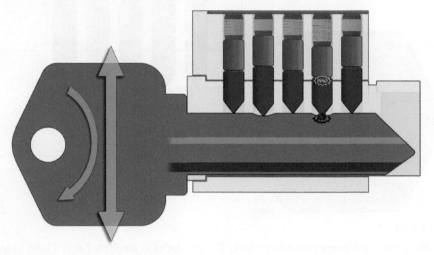

FIGURE 1.29

With pin stack #4 binding, attempts to wiggle the key up and down will cause the red key pin in position #4 to rub against the blade of the key.

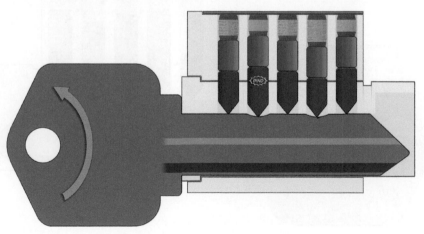

FIGURE 1.30

Counter-clockwise pressure on the key causes pin stack #2 to bind, just as it did before.

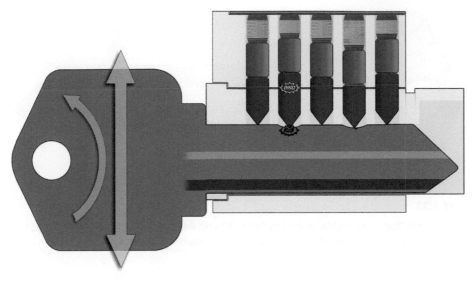

FIGURE 1.31

With pin stack #2 binding, attempts to wiggle the key up and down will cause the red key pin in position #2 to rub against the blade of the key.

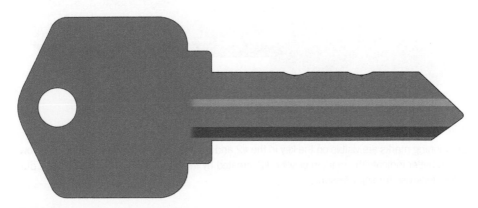

FIGURE 1.32

Impressioning marks are visible on the key in the #2 and #4 positions.

After this second pass of turning and wiggling, the key is removed and inspected again. Marks from the binding and rubbing should still be identifiable (see Figure 1.32). Much like before, these marks will likely be small and hard to see (see Figures 1.33 and 1.34 for arrows that help indicate where the marks are).

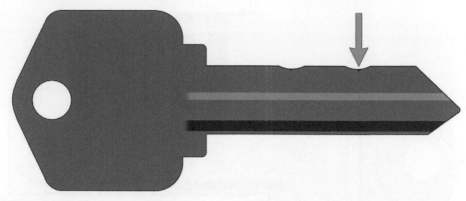

FIGURE 1.33

Impressioning marks are visible on the key in the #2 and #4 positions. In this figure, a green arrow serves to better indicate the mark in position #4, created by the wiggling which was performed during clockwise turning pressure.

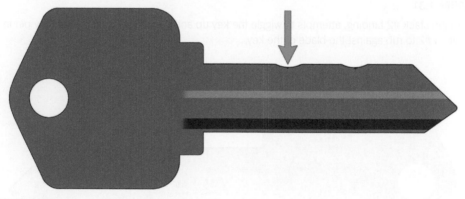

FIGURE 1.34

Impressioning marks are visible on the key in the #2 and #4 positions. In this figure, a green arrow serves to better indicate the mark in position #2, created by the wiggling which was performed during counter-clockwise turning pressure.

As was described earlier in this chapter, marks like this are an indication of pin stacks that are not in the proper position. We don't yet know anything at all about the other pin stacks in the lock, but we can tell from these impressioning marks that positions #2 and #4 on the key are not currently cut to the proper depth. Therefore, some more material is removed from the key in those positions (see Figure 1.35).

Again, the key is re-inserted into the lock, as shown in Figure 1.36. Something important has now happened, however. Pay particular attention

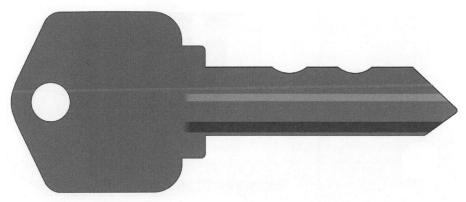

FIGURE 1.35

The key is filed further down in positions #2 and #4, since the marks made during the last pass of impressioning movements indicate that those two positions are still experiencing binding.

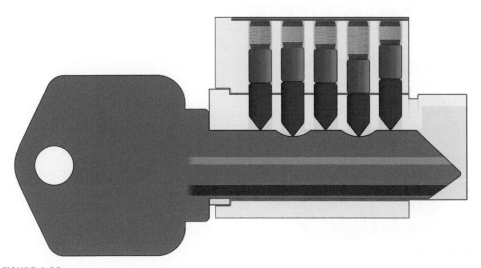

FIGURE 1.36

After this latest round of filing, the key is inserted into the lock again. Something significant has happened, however... can you tell what that is?

to the various positions of the pin stacks. Can you see the significant detail? Figure 1.37 will help you with another arrow, if need be. The repeated filing on the blade of the key has now moved one of the pin stacks into the proper position. The pins in position #4 are now raised to the same height to which the proper key would have lifted them had it been inserted into the lock.

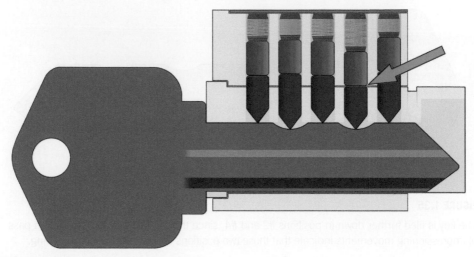

FIGURE 1.37

At this time, the pins in stack #4 are raised to the exact right height… that is, the height to which the proper key would have lifted them.

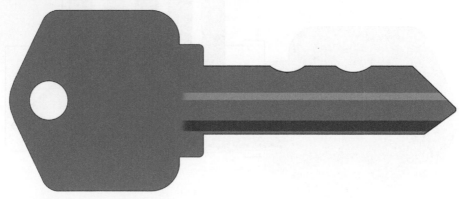

FIGURE 1.38

After the latest round of turning and wiggling, the key now shows marks that are appearing in somewhat different positions.

Because the pins in position #4 are at the correct height, they are *not* likely to bind if an attempt is made to rotate the plug. Thus, if the key is again turned and wiggled up-and-down, the pins in position #4 should not bind and therefore they should not make any marks on the blade of the key in that spot.

Imagine that this action has been taken. Imagine that another round of turning and wiggling has been performed in each direction and the key is removed and inspected. It is quite likely that one might see something akin to what is shown in Figure 1.38. The mark in position #2 (usually associated

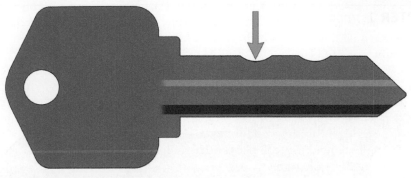

FIGURE 1.39

The mark in position #2 has appeared again, indicating that this pin stack is still binding.

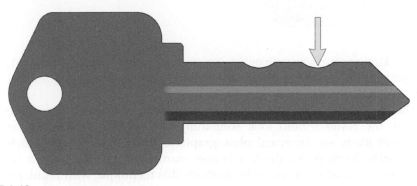

FIGURE 1.40

The mark in position #4 has ceased to re-appear. That is an indication that this pin stack may be in the proper position at this cut depth on the key blade.

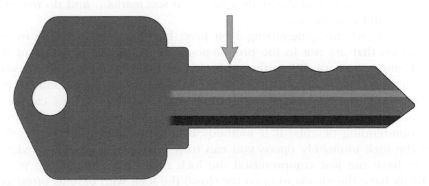

FIGURE 1.41

An entirely new mark has appeared in a spot that was previously untouched. This indicates where a different pin stack may now be binding. (In this case, it appears to be the pins in position #1.)

with counter-clockwise rotation of the key) is still visible (see Figure 1.39). The mark that had been appearing in position #4 (associated with clockwise rotation of the key) has failed to re-appear (see Figure 1.40). However, an entirely *new* mark is now showing up, this time in position #1 (see Figure 1.41).

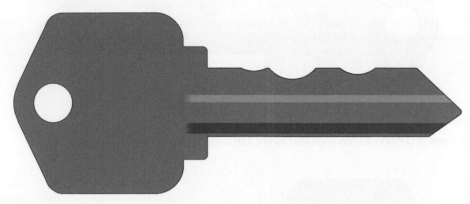

FIGURE 1.42

Some more filing results in a key with various cuts at different depths. Most likely, the cut that has been made in position #4 will not be made any deeper throughout the rest of the process.

If the key is again filed some more in these positions where marks have appeared, the result should look something like what is seen in Figure 1.42. As you will likely see in actual photographs later in this chapter which show impressioning in progress, the key is now starting to take shape in a way that will become familiar to people who perform this technique with regularity.

File marks when you see them, don't file when you don't

In a nutshell, the entire impressioning process can be summarized with the directive, "File the key in positions where you see marks... and do *not* file the key if you fail to see marks."

Of course, we are generalizing a bit here, but that is truly the heart of the matter. Pins that are not in the proper position are pins that will bind if you apply turning pressure. When those binding pins leave marks, it is possible to see directly on the blade of the key (without any need to disassemble the lock or inspect it internally) where pins are binding. Over time, a key can be filed down and fashioned in such a way as to ease the various pin stacks into their ideal, non-binding heights. It is methodical and sometimes tedious work, but when the lock ultimately opens you can truly celebrate a significant victory... for you have not just compromised the lock on that one occasion, you now effectively have the means to open (or close) the lock with ease as often as you wish because you have produced a working key.

TIPS AND TRICKS

It is my hope that the explanation of the mechanics of impressioning as described in the previous section is easy to understand and that you now have a decent grasp of how things should function when you try this yourself.

Of course, in actuality nothing is ever so neat and clean as it first appears on the pages of any educational text… and impressioning is no different. There are many ways that things may not go smoothly when this tactic is tried on locks that are encountered in the real world. Hopefully, the advice contained in this section will give you some extra help when you try impressioning in the field.

Seeing the mark is hard!

The first thing that most people say when they make their first few attempts at impressioning tends to be along the lines of, "I believed you when you said the marks would be hard to see, but I didn't fully appreciate *just how difficult* it would be to spot them." Often, the small rub marks that appear on the blade of a key during impressioning look like little more than blemishes or scuffs from production or simple handling. While blank keys might look shiny and smooth at first glance, their surface is actually quite uneven. Figure 1.43 is an image of the top edge of the blade of a key, as seen through a microscope. As you can imagine, attempting to discern one particular mark amid all of those ripples and ridges is a task no one would envy.

FIGURE 1.43

The blade of a blank key, viewed through a microscope. The surface is considerably uneven, due to how the metal is produced and plated.

Prepare your work surface

Before you begin any attempt at impressioning, it is essential that you properly prepare the blank key that you plan to use. The most common means of doing this is by filing or sanding the blank so that its top edge (where you will be looking for marks and filing cuts) is uniform. The key word here is "uniform" as opposed to "perfect" or even "smooth"… many times, the only tool that people will have available during impressioning is a hand file. Even though impressioning files tend to be quite fine, their teeth are large and rough enough to make it impossible to create anything akin to a high-polish, mirror-like surface on the edge of the key blade. This is perfectly alright. As long as you use your file to make the surface *consistent* you will then be able to identify any *inconsistent* marks which appear upon the façade that you have prepared. Look at the two images in Figure 1.44, showing a key blade that was prepared with a hand file. While the surface certainly could not be called "smooth" at least it is uniform. All of the filing marks are running in the same direction and they are of approximately the same intensity. (The fact that the user has chosen to file at a slight angle will also help, given that the insertion and removal of

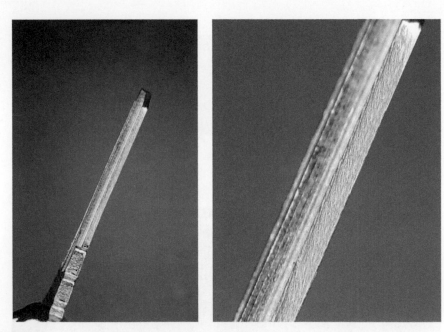

FIGURE 1.44

A blank key that has been prepared for impressioning. The surface still shows visible marks, but they are all now consistent and parallel, allowing the user to identify new marks which may appear when binding pins rub against the key.

the key may produce the occasional errant drag mark, but this will be directly down the length of the key and thus it will also stand out as unique and easily noticed.) Again, the key in this photo was prepared simply by using the flat side of a hand file. Fine grain sand paper will naturally produce even better results, if you are willing to spend the necessary time to use it.

TIP

Although it might seem like an interesting idea, do not get too fancy when it comes to preparing your blank keys prior to impressioning. I have seen many people attempt to "improve" upon the process by using power tools, such as rotary tools equipped with buffing tips, in the hopes of generating a high-gloss surface. While this does tend to produce very smooth metal, it is exceedingly difficult to hold the key steady during this process, and the results are often very inconsistent and uneven (see Figure 1.45).

One time my associates and I had the inspired idea to acquire a used rock tumbler from a junk sale, thinking we could load it full of blank keys and polishing grit and let it run for a week's time. Imagine our surprise when after days of continuous operation, we opened the rotating drum to reveal a load of keys whose finish had been totally stripped off and which looked like they had been sitting in the bottom of a riverbed or storm drain for the better part of a year (see Figure 1.46).

Stick with a hand file or sandpaper… or use the tactic which will be discussed in the next section, if you have access to a code-cutting key machine.

FIGURE 1.45

An attempt was made to polish the edge of this key using a Dremel hand tool. The result was indeed shiny, but it was far too uneven and wavy to be useful during impressioning.

FIGURE 1.46

These keys were placed in a rock tumbler in an attempt to make their surface smooth and even all over. It did not work as intended. Seriously… don't try this. :-)

Using specially-marked keys

While all of the previous advice is perfectly sound and will serve you well if you are using off-the-shelf blanks, I must admit that my impressioning work became considerably easier once I started using specially prepared keys. It is possible to add some particular features to your blank keys which will make the whole process of identifying marks and filing down far less complicated and eliminate a great deal of headache. Far and away, the best thing I ever did for myself when I started assembling a kit of supplies for impressioning was to prepare large quantities of "0-cut" keys.

Not everyone has access to a code-cutting key machine. However, if you can befriend someone who owns one or rent time on one or even just purchase keys from someone who will prepare them especially for you by using one, you will soon see what wonderful help they are (see Figure 1.47).

The user of a code-cutting key machine inputs the bitting code they wish to produce by means of a small numeric keypad, and then the machine will produce a key to that specification. While this is typically something that locksmiths will do when they wish to create a fresh, first-generation key for a customer, it is also possible to input codes that would normally never be used for a lock in the field and generate keys for other purposes. (Bump keys, for

FIGURE 1.47

This Ilco UltraCode machine is owned by The Open Organisation Of Lockpickers and it has been used to produce 0-cut keys for impressioning workshops at many Lockpick Village events.

example, are also sometimes known as "9-9-9" keys because inputting a code of all 9's on a code-cutting key machine will often generate them successfully, at least in situations where "9" is the manufacturer's deepest depth setting. We will discuss bump keys further in Chapter 4.)

If you wish to prepare the ideal key for impressioning, you would often be well-served by repeatedly keying a value of zero into a code-cutting key machine. Now, technically, a depth of zero should mean "no cut" but this does not mean that the high-speed cutting wheel will *completely fail to contact* the key as it moves along its work path. In fact, in all instances when I have tried this, cutting a key to all zero values will result in what you can see in Figure 1.48 (compare it with a perfectly blank key as seen in Figure 1.49).

As you can see, a zero-cut key will indeed be contacted by the cutting wheel in each bitting position. The contact will be minimal, a very light grazing is all, but that is enough to produce very distinct notches on the key blade (see Figure 1.50). These notches serve two fantastic functions. First, if the key machine is well-maintained and has a sharp cutting wheel, these notches tend to be very high-polish surfaces which make seeing impressioning marks much easier. Second, the notches serve as ideal "spacing" indicators, which will reduce

FIGURE 1.48

A key that has been cut to a value of "zero" in all bitting positions by means of a code-cutting key machine. Compare it with the completely blank key seen in Figure 1.49.

FIGURE 1.49

A completely blank key that has not been prepared in any way. Compare it with the zero-cut key seen in Figure 1.48.

FIGURE 1.50

A highly-magnified view of the blade of a key after it has been cut to a bitting code of all zeros in an Ilco UltraCode key machine. Compare what is seen here with the photograph in Figure 1.43 to see the difference that this makes.

the overall searching that you are likely to do when looking for an impressioning mark. If you know the specific places on the blade of the key where pins *should* be touching, you don't need to spend your time searching all over the rest of the key looking for tiny marks where pins would *never* be touching.

Figure 1.51 is a highly magnified view of a zero-cut key, showing an impressioning mark exactly where one would expect it to appear: directly in the middle of one of the small zero-cut notches on the edge of the key blade.

One other way in which I have found it helpful to prepare keys for impressioning is to draw a series of vertical lines down the flat side of the key with a felt-tipped marker, as a way to prevent people from "drifting" fore or aft along the key blade as they file down. When you're simply making shallow cuts all near the top edge of the key (and when you have a whole row of zero-cut notches providing you with excellent spacing measurements) it is relatively easy to control your filing and cut straight down into the key. Once you've cut a quarter inch or more into the blade, however, it is not uncommon to take a step back and suddenly notice that you've "drifted" considerably away from a line that is plumb and true.

Whenever I am starting someone out with a zero-cut key on their initial attempts at impressioning, I draw black lines down the edge of the key underneath each spot that has been marked by the cutting machine. Figure 1.52 shows a key that has been prepared in this manner.

FIGURE 1.51

Using a zero-cut key, impressioning marks become much easier to spot. They have a uniform, polished surface on which to appear, and these notched areas of the key serve as useful guides enabling the user to look in just the right places when searching for marks after turning and wiggling the key in a lock.

FIGURE 1.52

Drawing vertical lines down the broad side of a key blade will help to ensure that filed cuts do not drift out of position during the act of impressioning.

Lighting and magnification

Many would argue that while it can be beneficial to prepare your key prior to impressioning, even more universally accepted is the notion that properly *illuminating* and *magnifying* the key during impressioning makes an even more significant impact. I agree that it is hard to over-emphasize just how useful proper lamps and optics are throughout this process.

Until you have seen the phenomenon yourself, it may be difficult for you to appreciate how the small marks created during impressioning can seem to "appear" or completely "disappear" depending only on factors such as the angle at which a light is shining on the key or the direction in which you are looking. Figures 1.53 and 1.54 illustrate this trend. They are two images of the exact same key being held at two distinct angles. Notice how the small impressioning mark (in bitting position #2, approximately one-half inch from the key's shoulder) is virtually invisible in the first image, but how it stands out quite clearly in the latter.

Many times, the problems of light shining from the "wrong angle" can be alleviated by using equipment which can bathe the key in light from all directions at once. The style of lamp most frequently preferred by people who are skilled at impressioning tends to be the magnifying lamp of the type seen in Figure 1.55. Popular for jewelry-making, hardware soldering, and a multitude of other activities where close inspection of small components is routine, these lamps are often the best way to inspect keys with significant magnification and omnidirectional light. Figure 1.56 shows a key as it appears when observed with the aid of this type of magnifying lamp.

The one detracting factor regarding these types of lamps is the fact that they are not particularly portable. They might work just fine for impressioning that is taking place on a tabletop at a sport-picking event or on a locksmith's workbench (or even in his or her mobile van), but if you are attempting to perform impressioning in the field—particularly if you are doing so covertly using only the equipment that you have carried with you in your pockets or in a small backpack—then something more compact is needed.

A few people whom I know have sourced inexpensive otoscopes from discount medical supply catalogs, and these seem to work in a pinch. When using these implements, one does not have much ability to easily view the key from various angles, however. Somewhat more effective are items known as "light boxes" which provide a wider angle view yet still tend to be small enough to be kept in a pocket or small tool case. These devices are either self-contained units with internal lighting or adapters designed to slip over the end of a mini flashlight (see Figure 1.57). In either style, however, common features that they share tend to be an observing window with a magnifying lens and a slot into which a key can be inserted.

Personally, when I'm on a penetration job and the space I have for equipment carried with me is at an absolute premium, I tend to always rely on a "mini magnifier" that my associate Babak discovered while traveling overseas.

FIGURE 1.53

A photograph of a key during impressioning. There is a small impressioning mark on the blade, but it is very difficult to see at this angle.

FIGURE 1.54

A photograph of the same key seen in Figure 1.53, held at a different angle. The small impressioning mark on the blade stands out rather clearly when viewed from this perspective.

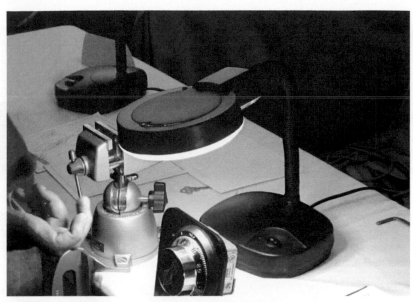

FIGURE 1.55

An illuminating magnifier lamp being used in an impressioning training classroom.

FIGURE 1.56

Impressioning a key is far easier with the aid of a magnifying lamp. Notice how we can not only see the mark left by a pin, but even its small "drag trail" can be observed where the pin scratched as the key was being removed.

FIGURE 1.57

A light box produced by Lishi Tools and a magnifying flashlight adapter produced by MB USA. Security professionals often criticize the Lishi box due to minor flaws in its construction, but both of these devices are capable of providing substantial help in identifying marks on the key during impressioning. *(Photos by UAP Limited and Barry Wels.)*

FIGURE 1.58

This mini magnifier light is my favorite impressioning aid when I'm performing a penetration test. It is highly concealable and still provides sufficient magnification and illumination to see marks on the blade of a key.

Shown in Figure 1.58, this terrific little tool is unbelievably compact. When stored in its closed position, it is only about 1¼ inches square! When it comes time to observe something closely, however, the mini magnifier snaps open and features a sliding optic which provides varying focus. There is even a built-in LED light powered by watch batteries.

This little tool is capable of an astonishing forty-five power magnification, which more than makes up for the fact that the light source is not as omni-directional as I would ideally like. I have experimented with augmenting the small clear plastic ring seen in the photos in Figure 1.58 to make the illumination more useful during impressioning. Using a 3D printer I have been able to fashion supplemental rings of plastic that help to diffuse and soften the light from the magnifier's LED unit.

While I have not seen this particular tool in any locksmith catalogs, The CORE Group does make it available to students in our Advanced Physical Penetration Testing course and it is also available on the web at http://enterthecore.net.

One final remark that I should make about illumination concerns the use of ultraviolet light as an impressioning aid. In a nutshell, some people swear by UV light while others dislike it. Actually, I should clarify that statement somewhat… what many individuals dislike about ultraviolet illumination during impressioning is the use of *UV-reactive ink* from a special pen or marker. Some locksmiths feel that a terrific way to see impressioning marks more clearly is to paint a line of UV-reactive ink along the edge of your key. It is true that this often makes the marks stand out more prominently, when viewed with the appropriate lighting. However, in my experience, after one or two passes in and out of the lock, the ink will tend to get smudged and smeared all over the pins, resulting in an unhelpful blur of glowing stripes all over the key as you continue to work.

As with most things in the lockpicking and lock-opening world, my mantra is, "Try it for yourself and see how you like it." If any specific tactic works for you, far be it from me to tell you that it's the "wrong" way to do something. However, I personally do not use ultraviolet lighting when performing impressioning attacks.

More tips for spotting the mark

As was already emphasized at the beginning of this section, it is often quite difficult to see the marks that binding pins will leave on the key during impressioning. Hopefully, some additional photographs will be able to convey further details of exactly what kinds of marks you will hope to see and how they will appear when you try impressioning yourself.

Figures 1.59 through 1.61 show a key during the impressioning of a Corbin lock. Notice how the mark is easy to see when the key is held in one direction, but very difficult to see when the light strikes from a different angle. Also, notice how the mark itself is not "centered" on the blade of the key. This is because as the filing cut grew deeper down the key, the metal being contacted by the pin was further and further to one side.

Sometimes the key pins within a lock will not have sharp, pointed tips where they contact a key. This is particularly common with "no name" or store-brand locks, whose pins may be only slightly rounded on each end. (These pins are designed to be reversible, in order to ease the process of automated production on an assembly line.) In locks such as this, the impressioning mark sometimes will not appear like a small dot or scratch but rather more like a divot or dent on the blade of your key. The photographs in Figures 1.62 through 1.65 show a key with a subtle, dent-like mark.

TIP

The key seen in Figures 1.62 through 1.65 may look slightly different from ones you have seen in previous photographs. That is because it is not a zero-cut key, but rather a blank that was fed into a code-cutting key machine into which the code 1-1-1-1-1 was input. Sometimes this is a popular tactic during impressioning competitions where speed is of the essence. A series of one-cut notches on the key will highlight and provide spacing just as effectively as a series of zero-cut notches, but it saves time by having some material already removed from the key in each bitting position.

After all, it is virtually unheard of for any real-world locks to ever be pinned with a value of "zero" in *any* position. Each cut on the blade of a key will in reality always be *at least* at a depth of "one" or greater. Therefore, a few people choose to save time by using "one-cut" keys during impressioning. Personally, I always opt to start with zero-cut keys... because you never really know, there's always the one-in-a-million chance that some screwball bitting combination is being used in a particular lock system and one position may actually have to remain at the blank key height.

A particularly useful technique for accurately identifying marks on the key as you impression a lock involves using your magnification and illumination tools *before* you turn and wiggle the key in the lock... not just after you do so. Allow me to clarify. Many people will opt to proceed with impressioning as follows: they insert their key, turn and wiggle it, remove the key, look through their magnifier for marks, file a bit, then re-insert the key into the lock and repeat the process. I feel that this omits a very critical step in the process.

I believe the best way to proceed with impressioning (after you have prepared your blank key) is to *first and foremost* look at the key with proper magnification and illumination, *before* you ever insert it into the lock. Get a feel for how the whole key appears. Take note of any areas that appear blemished

FIGURE 1.59

This key is being used to impression a Corbin lock. The impressioning mark is appearing directly in the bottom of the current filing cut, but it is off to one side of the key because the metal at this depth is not directly centered underneath the pin.

or discolored. Become accustomed to how the key looks at different angles. Only then—once you have gotten a fair sense of how the key looks *without any marks*—should you attempt to insert, turn, and wiggle the key. Then, when you remove it and observe it closely again, it should be possible to notice marks that were not there before... no matter how slight they may be. The same rule applies after you file the key down in any position... *before you insert it back into the lock* you should look at it again with magnification under proper light. Look at the surface which you just created using your hand file. Is it clean? Are there any new scratches or areas of inconsistency that you might incorrectly identify as an impressioning mark? If there are, take the time to clean them up with one or two more soft, even passes from your file in an attempt to polish the key in that spot. (Or, at the very least, simply make a mental note of any small imperfections left by your file so that you can rule them out when you search for impressioning marks later on.)

Ultimately, if at any time during an attempt at impressioning you are *unsure* if you are seeing a "true" mark or not, **do not file deeper in that position.** Simply use one or two very soft, even passes with your file in an effort to smooth the surface of the key and then see if the mark returns in that position more clearly after additional turning and wiggling of the key.

FIGURE 1.60

The same exact impressioning mark seen clearly in Figure 1.59 is now much harder to discern when the key is held at a different angle.

FIGURE 1.61

When the key is held at this angle, the light catches it in such a way that the impressioning mark—which was clearly visible in Figure 1.59 and still slightly visible in Figure 1.60—is totally obscured.

FIGURE 1.62

This key has been turned and wiggled in a lock. The impressioning mark that was left by a pin is very hard to see.

FIGURE 1.63

This is the same key as the one shown in Figure 1.62. The impressioning mark is just barely visible at this angle.

FIGURE 1.64

Now with the key held at a different angle and the light hitting it more directly, the small "dent-like" impressioning mark is somewhat visible. If you cannot discern it, see Figure 1.65.

FIGURE 1.65

A green arrow indicates the location of the impressioning mark on this key. Notice how it is not a small dot or scratch, but rather almost a kind of small "dent" in the blade of the key. This is due to the non-pointed shape of the key pins in this particular lock.

Some advice concerning filing

Let us focus briefly on the topic of filing. Having a good filing technique and taking care to make your cuts in a consistent and even manner, avoiding some common problems, can often be the difference between opening a lock using one or two keys and opening a lock using half a dozen keys or more.

How much to file

When you identify marks on your key during impressioning and you are confident that they are the result of binding pins, it is necessary to file on that position of the key. Ideally, you would want to file the key down to the next manufacturer-specified cut depth. In most instances, this means cuts will deepen by approximately $1/40^{th}$ or $1/50^{th}$ of an inch each time. (The bulk of lock manufacturers use bitting depth increments between 0.02 and 0.03 inches, although some unique models of lock have bitting differentials that are far smaller, sometimes as little as 0.015 or 0.012 inches.)

Unfortunately, it is often quite difficult to estimate depths of such a small degree without the aid of measuring tools (see Figure 1.66). Some individuals opt to use locksmith "decoder cards" which are available from supply catalogs and online at relatively low cost (see Figure 1.67). However, because these types of cards tend to be created specifically for certain brands and models of

FIGURE 1.66

Here we see a key being filed during the process of impressioning. The key was originally code-cut to a bitting depth of one in each pin position, and now position #3 has been manually filed to a bitting depth of two.

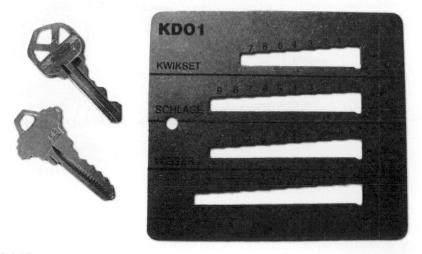

FIGURE 1.67

A key decoding depth card, available from most locksmithing supply catalogs and web sites.

locks (since different manufacturers frequently use different-sized pins), some people choose to rely instead on callpers for measuring. Calipers—along with a depth chart specific to the brand of lock that you are impressioning—will usually help you to execute your cuts at more or less the proper depth each time. While most people picture a sliding-ruler type of tool when they hear the word *caliper,* one of the world's most noted lock impressioning masters, Jos Weyers, is a fan of "dial"-style calipers when he is working. He has even gone so far as to augment the face plate on the measuring gauge of his Kroeplin-brand dial caliper with tick marks that indicate manufacturer-specific cut depths (see Figure 1.68). Students in CORE Group advanced training classes that concern impressioning are issued a thickness gauge pocket caliper which can perform this same function (see Figure 1.69). This compact tool is also part of our equipment kits on physical penetration tests, and is available on The CORE Group web site at http://enterthecore.net.

WARNING

If you choose to use any measuring tools during the process of impressioning, take care to ensure that they do not mar or scuff the surface of the key blade when you take your measurements. Such spots left on the key could be mistaken for impressioning marks if you are not careful. Always remember to closely inspect your key *before* you insert it into the lock, not just after you have removed it!

FIGURE 1.68

The Kroeplin brand dial caliper used by Jos Weyers when he is impressioning locks. Note the additional markings that have been added to the dial; they indicate manufacturer-specific cut depths for a particular brand of locks. *(Photo courtesy of Dennis van Zuijlekom.)*

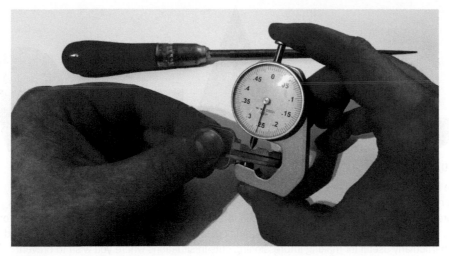

FIGURE 1.69

The pocket caliper tool issued during CORE Group trainings and employed by CORE Group operatives on physical penetration tests when impressioning or master key escalation attacks are performed.

File types and shapes

There are a variety of files popular for use during impressioning. While most lock-smiths and security professionals will agree that files made for the jewelry industry tend to perform better than others (Grobet Swiss brand products are particularly acclaimed), there is plenty of variance concerning what *shape* of file people most prefer. Round and half-round files are the types that I most typically encounter among my friends and associates. When impressioning, a rounded shape is ideal for your cut because it allows for slight drift and off-center filing while still allowing marks to appear on an even, smooth surface. Having a flat file available to you is quite useful, as well, since this will help you prepare the surface of your blank keys if they have not already been sanded or marked with code-cut notches. The half-round file shape incorporates both curved and flat surfaces in a single package.

Fully-round files are also popular among individuals who do not wish to be encumbered by a need to orient their file each time they pick it up (many competitive lock impressioners choose fully-round files for this very reason, to save precious seconds during sporting sessions). Other people choose to adapt a fully-round file in such a way as to make one side slightly dull while keeping the other side sharp, thus allowing for deep cutting and also for smoothing and polishing with the same tool.

Many locksmith catalogs will also offer more exotic shapes of files. The most popular file in a non-regular shape is called a pippin. This shape's profile appears almost teardrop-like, and it is designed to aid people in making wide, sloping edges to their cuts. In a moment, we will further examine the notion of how to shape the cuts you make upon a key while filing. If I had a machine

FIGURE 1.70

The first three images in this diagram represent the most typical file shapes used during impressioning. From left to right: half-round, fully-round, pippin. The subsequent two images represent file shapes which I have never seen in the real world, but which I hope could exist one day. From left to right: wide trough, flat-bottom angled notch. The "wide trough" design would be particularly useful for making impressioning cuts in situations where you wish to prevent new students of this skill accidentally "canyoning" their cuts (a predicament described in an upcoming section) and the "flat-bottom angled notch" would be useful for Master Key Escalation attacks (the focus of Chapter 3).

shop capable of producing files, I know that I would fabricate a few unique designs which I have never seen available. These concept files appear next to the standard shapes I have just described in a side-by-side comparison in Figure 1.70.

Filing technique

When you are filing your key during impressioning, pay particular attention to how you are positioning the file. Do your best to maintain a "flat" orientation with your tools as you prepare and then later as you cut into the key. Do not "roll" the file across and try to avoid creating slanted or sloped cuts. Some people advocate use of an "angled" filing method, as a means to make the edge of the key's blade into a sharper, thinner surface area. The thinking is that this thin surface area will have less strength and thus will be more likely to mark or dent during impressioning. While this may be a somewhat useful technique for impressioning wafer locks (which is not being discussed here) I find it to be counter-productive when impressioning pin tumbler locks... all it does is reduce the overall surface area where pins might make contact, thus obscuring already hard-to-find marks. Figure 1.71 should hopefully give a better picture of the type of filing I advocate during impressioning.

WARNING

Be aware that most files are produced with teeth that are designed to cut in one direction, not both. Almost all files (particularly those sold for use during impressioning) are designed to remove material by being pushed *away* from the user. The reverse motion, drawing the file *back toward* the user, is usually not to be attempted while pressing a file down upon the medium being cut. Doing this (filing *toward yourself* against the normal cutting direction) will cause excess wear on the teeth and cause the file to dull prematurely.

Some individuals do choose to intentionally dull their file, but this is usually done in a controlled manner and often only on one side (usually on one half of a fully-round file, in order to create a dual-purpose tool that can either remove lots of material or be used to gently polish away scuff marks). Most high quality impressioning files cost $30 to $60 USD, sometimes even more if you are looking to acquire exotic shapes like the teardrop pippin style. Safeguard your investment by cleaning your file regularly and by only filing in one direction, away from yourself. (And be sure to keep an eye on anyone else who might borrow your file for a moment, to ensure that they know this rule before they start trying to impression by themselves!)

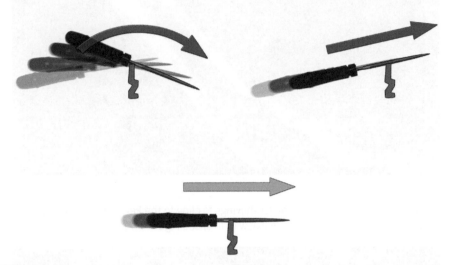

FIGURE 1.71

This series of three diagrams illustrates various filing techniques. On the upper-left is what could be described as a "roll" across the key, shifting direction as you swipe with the file in order to create a rounded top surface. I do not recommend this in any situation. On the upper right is an image showing a file being used at an angle. I do not recommend this either when impressioning pin tumbler locks. The diagram in the middle at the bottom shows the technique that I advocate: an even, flat application of the file directly across the edge of the key. In my opinion, this gives you good cutting ability and also leaves behind a surface that is uniform, predictable, repeatable, and therefore well suited for seeing additional impressioning marks.

Maintain a clean work area

Filing keys during impressioning will generate a lot of small metal shavings. Most of these will just fall aside, but some will cling to the key... particularly right where the cutting is happening (see Figures 1.72 and 1.73). Take care to scrape these filings from the key using a fingernail or any other non-metallic implement which will not scratch the key itself. Also do your best to wipe or blow all of the small metal filings off the key before you re-insert it into the lock for your next pass of turning and wiggling. There will always be more than enough stray debris in the lock causing confusion in the search

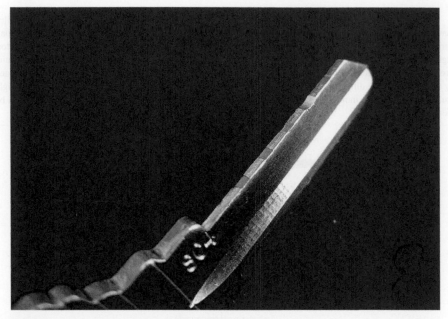

FIGURE 1.72

During filing, it is common for small metal shavings to cling to the key, particularly on the edge where the blade is being cut. For a better view of this, see Figure 1.73.

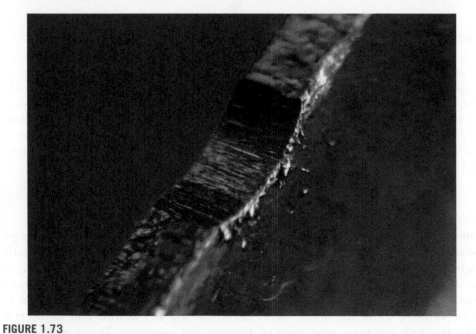

FIGURE 1.73

A magnified image of the key seen in Figure 1.72, this image illustrates all of the superfluous crud and waste filings that often cling to the key during impressioning. Be sure to clean these off frequently.

for impressioning marks; there is no need to add to this situation by failing to clean the key regularly as you work.

Take care to avoid "canyoning"

Perhaps the biggest problem that my students encounter during training courses when they are filing keys is accidentally "canyoning" their cuts. My first book, *Practical Lock Picking,* briefly mentioned a consideration with which locksmiths must contend with frequently… something known in the trade as Maximum Adjacent Cut Specification (MACS). This topic will also be raised in Chapter 3 of this book, which discusses privilege escalation within master-keyed systems. The essence of this pertains to the fact that the cuts on a key should never be sloped too steeply. Cuts that are too deep with very steep side-walls can "trap" pins within them and prevent the key from being removed… hardly something you wish to have happen if you are attempting to covertly attack a lock without the owner recognizing that anything is taking place!

Figure 1.74 shows a key that became badly stuck in a lock due to how it was filed. With a good deal of shaking and rapping, I was fortunately able to get the key back out again and photograph it as an example of what not to do. (This was only possible because the lock was not mounted in a door but

FIGURE 1.74

A key which had become badly stuck in a lock due to "canyoning" of the side walls on the filed cuts. Notice how this key could be smoothly inserted into the lock, with the pins easily riding up on the front slope of the key, but then the pin stacks would drop into the deep filed cuts and become trapped, in effect jamming the key in the lock.

instead was simply a loose training cylinder that could be turned in various directions and struck against the tabletop.)

Impressioning handles

In addition to a blank key, a file, and a good source of magnification and illumination, the final tool you will use when impressioning a lock is a handle with which to hold and manipulate the key. As was stated earlier in this chapter, the turning force used when binding the pins stacks is quite considerable... *far* more than the kind of turning pressure used when picking a lock. It is almost never possible to adequately make impressioning marks on a key simply by holding it in your bare hands. Special handles are used in order to turn with great force and wiggle up and down adequately.

Locksmithing catalogs and online suppliers often sell impressioning handles. They tend to be plastic and feature a few set screws with which to grip blank keys. A typical, name-brand impressioning handle can be seen in Figure 1.75. As you might imagine, however, hardcore enthusiasts and locksporters tend to custom-make their own hardware. Jos Weyers likes to rely on a handle that was milled out of a solid billet of aluminum (see Figure 1.76). Featuring a long side bar with which to achieve maximum torque, this tool does a great job of holding the key firmly and also turning it in order to bind the pins. It is typical to catch

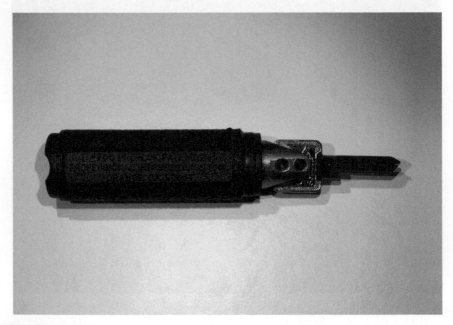

FIGURE 1.75

A traditional impressioning handle, produced by Pro-Lock and available through most any locksmith supply catalog. *(Photo courtesy of Dennis van Zuijlekom.)*

a glimpse of this tool in videos of Jos breaking world records during impressioning competitions. In my own penetration testing toolkit I keep my own custom-
made impressioning handle (see Figure 1.77). It was crafted by a member of the
German sport-picking group Sportsfreunde der Sperrtechnik (SSDeV) and given
to me at the LockCon conference. I absolutely love this impressioning handle. It

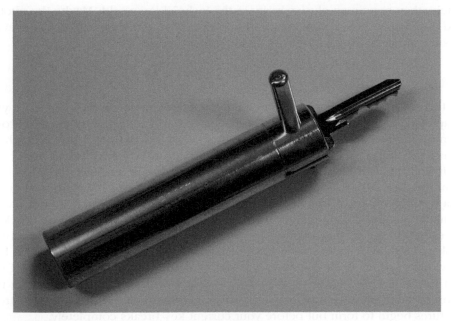

FIGURE 1.76
The impressioning handle used by world-champion Jos Weyers. This tool is produced by Jord
Knaap (http://www.kjs-tools.com). Note the solid metal construction and long side peg used to
help turn the key with great force. *(Photo courtesy of Dennis van Zuijlekom.)*

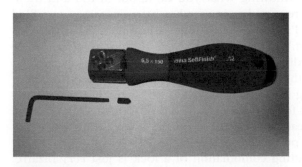

FIGURE 1.77
My impressioning handle, made by a member of the German sport-picking group SSDeV. Note the
substantial number of pointed set screws which bite into the key from both sides. It is rumored
that tools such as this may begin to appear on the site http://spyland.de when it is completed.

features *eight* separate set screws, each of which is particularly long (with more than a quarter inch of threads for maximum strength) and each pointed at the tip (for the best possible bite into the key). Designed from a Wiha screwdriver handle, this tool feels terrific in my hand and has never let me down in the field. If this fellow ever decides to mass-produce these I would think they would easily be the finest impressioning handles to hit the market. For now, unfortunately, they remain an elusive rarity in the lockpicking world. Maybe the photos and description here will inspire you to create your own custom tools, however, if you become a devotee of the tactic of impressioning.

If you run into trouble

All this talk of impressioning handles and the degree to which they can assist you in applying considerable turning force may give some indication of just how common it is to break a key when you are attempting this tactic. It's fine if this happens to you; it is perfectly normal and something from which you can recover.

If you break a key during an impressioning attempt, remove the key blade from the lock (using a key extractor tool, if necessary) and hold it directly next to a fresh blank key. Vice-Grips or pliers will often help you to keep both pieces of metal steady and in perfect alignment. Using a fine-tip permanent marker, trace the outline of the broken key upon the new blank, and then discard the broken piece and file the new key down to the bitting heights which you had previously achieved. Of course, it is easier to align and old and a new key if the first key is not yet broken… so be sure to keep an eye on your key during the impressioning process and consider performing this trade-off procedure if stress fractures begin to form but before your current key breaks completely.

One other difficulty that you might encounter is the suspicion that you have filed too deeply in one particular position. After all, if you overshoot the shear line between the key pin and the driver pin, impressioning marks will not magically cease to appear. A driver pin will bind and cause marking just as effectively as a key pin. Knowing what you do about MACS and traditional bitting combinations, there may be times when you examine your filed key and remark to yourself, "I'm still seeing impressioning marks, but this key simply does *not* look right." If that happens, use a similar technique to the one described above regarding broken keys… clamp a fresh key next to your current one and draw on the new key using a fine-tip permanent marker. Duplicate most of your existing cuts to the new key (perhaps cutting slightly shallower in each position, just for good measure) but do not make any cut at all in the position where you fear you may have gone too far during your first attempt. Figure 1.78 shows this process.

Sometimes, of course, the bitting combination of a lock is just *very* bizarre. Don't discount the possibility that the actual bitting code for a lock could incorporate a substantial degree of high/low variation from one position to the next. Of course, it also makes sense to usually *expect* simple bitting combinations, particularly in the North American market.

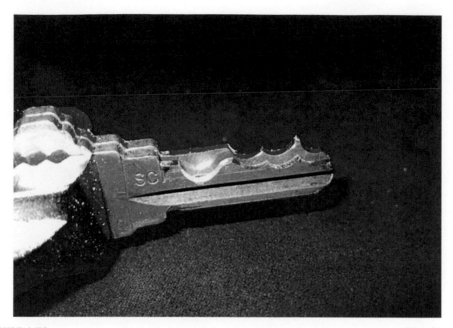

FIGURE 1.78

When you fear that one cut has perhaps become too deep on the key being impressioned, clamp a new key next to the original key and replicate the existing cuts onto this replacement key. Make each cut slightly shallower, and do not file at all in the position where you feared that a cut has proceeded well past the appropriate depth. The impressioning process should be able to proceed from this point forward in order to find each correct cut depth.

OPEN!

When you are successful with an impressioning attack, it is a remarkable feeling. Not only are you overwhelmed by the sudden rush that comes with the realization that the lock is opening, but you are then able to actually remove your hand-made key and inspect it. Unlike with lockpicking, where the tools that you remove from the lock are always the same tools that you had originally inserted, impressioning gives quite a thrill (at least it does for me) when you can actually look up on the fruits of your labor and see the working key in your hands (see Figure 1.79).

When you have gotten the plug to turn during an impressioning effort, you are 99% finished, but one last step remains. Turn the plug back and forth. Do you feel it rotating smoothly or is there drag? Remove the key and inspect it closely. Most likely, you will see evidence of "cratering" in at least one position. Sometimes a cut is not the exact right depth, but it is close enough for the lock to operate anyway (particularly if you are applying considerable turning pressure in an attempt to bind any remaining pins). When this happens, with the lock effectively being forced open, the soft brass of the key will experience

FIGURE 1.79

A photograph of the very first lock that I ever impressioned. I did this at a TOOOL meeting in Amsterdam years ago… you can bet I still have the key. :-)

a notable denting where a key pin might smash down. Photos of this phenomenon can be seen in Figures 1.80 and 1.81.

If you see any deep craters such as these on your keys when you successfully get a lock to open, revisit those positions with your file and remove just a little more material until the crater is gone and the plug turns smoothly.

NOTE

Bear in mind that just because a lock has opened and its plug is turning successfully after an impressioning attempt, this does not always guarantee that you have produced a key with a "real" bitting code for that lock. If the lock you were attacking was part of a master-keyed system, you may have hit a mix of master key and change key shear lines. The key you have may operate that lock, but it might not be the "true" key for that particular door. If you are servicing a lock where the original key has been lost and you know that you are dealing with a master-keyed system, use the key which you have hand-filed to open the door and then to remove and disassemble the lock, in order to inspect and measure each individual pin so that you might learn details of the mastering system and thus discover both the user's change key for this particular door as well as the top master key for the whole system. (This topic will become clearer once you have read Chatper Three which discusses master-keyed systems in greater detail.)

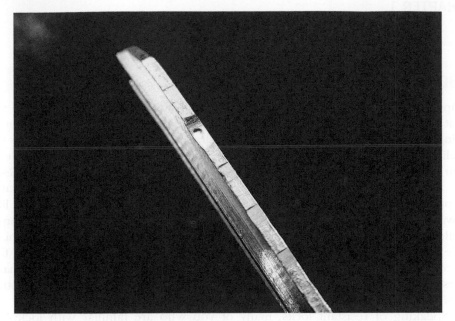

FIGURE 1.80

A key which turns in a lock without being cut to the exact perfect depth in every position will more than likely experience "cratering" in at least one spot. Note the deep, round impact point on the middle of this key blade.

FIGURE 1.81

A magnified image of the key seen in Figure 1.80. This type of "cratering" is a clear indication of a cut that came close to the perfect depth, but which was still just a little too shallow.

LOCKS THAT RESIST IMPRESSIONING

Impressioning is not an easy skill. All things considered, I believe it's fair to say that impressioning is a more difficult skill to acquire and use effectively than something like lockpicking. Perhaps the most frustrating part about impressioning is the feeling that you may not be succeeding. With little concrete evidence available to you while you're in the midst of the process, it is easy to get discouraged. Resist the temptation to give up! Figure 1.82 is a photo of a key that I had partially-impressioned during a penetration test. After five or ten minutes of filing, I felt like I wasn't accomplishing enough and decided to find another way into the target building. Later on, however, my team cracked the combination on a key-organizer safe and found the top master key for the whole facility. As you can see from this photo, I was closer to succeeding than I could have ever realized. Out of six chambers in the lock, I had successfully impressioned three of them, with the other positions well on their way to being successfully determined.

Speaking of resistant locks, many of you who are familiar with lockpicking may be aware of features that manufacturers will add to their products to

FIGURE 1.82

I stopped my impressioning attempt partway through the creation of this key. As you can see, I would have done well to continue on, since I had successfully found half of the master key's bitting positions and would have likely discovered the rest given just a little more time and effort.

frustrate attempts to use pick tools. Uniquely-shaped driver pins (known as spool pins, mushroom pins, and the like) are installed in locks sometimes. While these pins can make picking difficult, consider what effect they can have on impressioning. Figure 1.83 will give you some indication of what role they play... none at all.

This is not to say that there are no means by which lock manufacturers can attempt to prevent impressioning, however. Some locks feature specialized *key* pins that are shaped in a way which will make impressioning attacks very difficult. Figure 1.84 shows a lock constructed with one such pin. Known informally as a "torpedo" pin, this key pin is specifically designed to prevent binding when a blank key is inserted and turned.

Figures 1.85 through 1.92 document the manner in which torpedo pins can make impressioning very difficult, as your ability to bind the pin stack (and thus, your ability to mark the blade of the key) will decrease as the pin drops farther and farther into the plug.

It is still possible to impression a lock that incorporates torpedo pins, but it will usually involve a good deal of retracing one's steps, returning to file more in positions where you once thought you had conclusively found the correct depth. Often it is frustrating enough that an attacker will attempt to choose an alternative means of opening the lock or they will simply focus their efforts elsewhere.

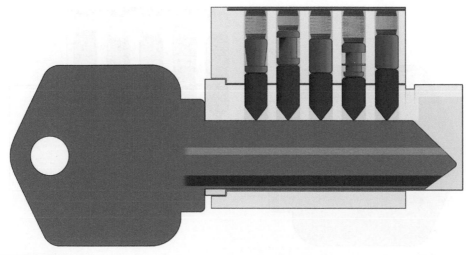

FIGURE 1.83

Because impressioning is an attack that forces the pin stacks to their maximum height, this means that any anti-pick driver pins will be forced completely out of the plug when the blank key is inserted. Specialized driver pins will play no role at all during the impressioning process.

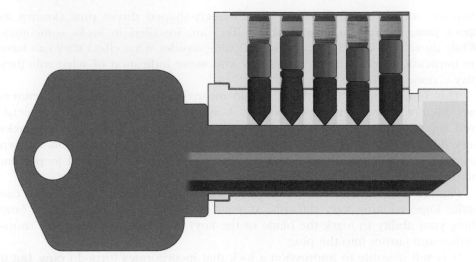

FIGURE 1.84

A lock equipped with an anti-impressioning "torpedo" key pin in the second chamber. The Swedish company ASSA likes to use pins such as these in their high-security locks.

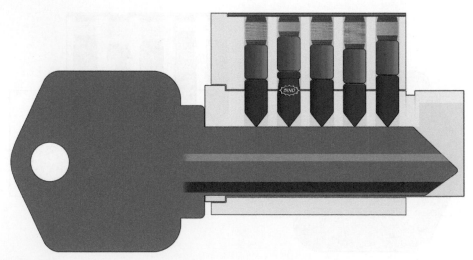

FIGURE 1.85

With the key turned to one side, the pin stack binds.

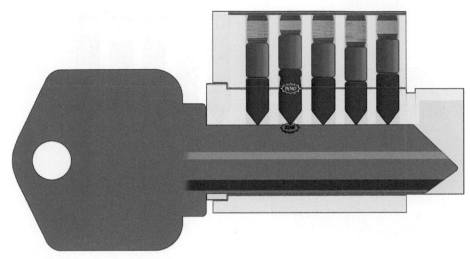

FIGURE 1.86

Wiggling the key up and down should produce rubbing and mark the key in this position.

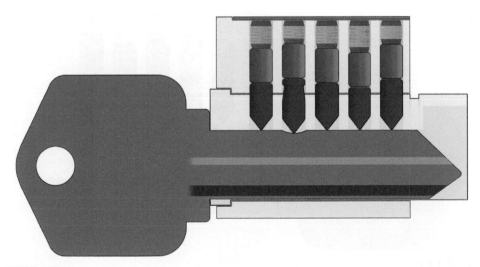

FIGURE 1.87

With an impressioning mark observed, the key is filed down slightly.

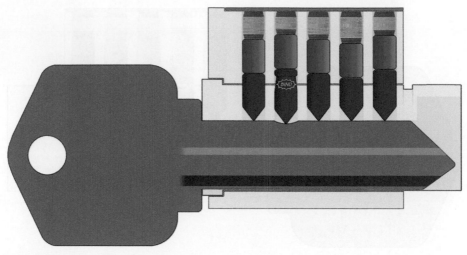

FIGURE 1.88

Now, since the narrow neck of the torpedo pin is starting to reach the shear line, the pin stack will bind less when the key is turned.

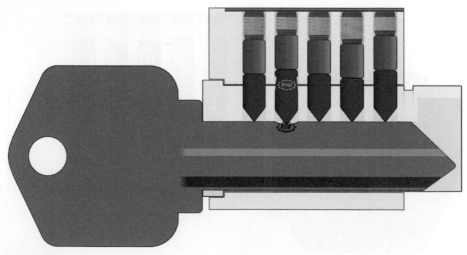

FIGURE 1.89

There is far less chance that the key will rub very much against the torpedo pin during wiggling. Very little in the way of a mark is likely to be left on the key blade.

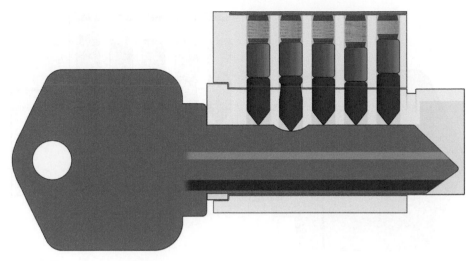

FIGURE 1.90

Assuming that someone is very skilled, perhaps they were able to see a small mark on the key blade, and they filed this position down yet again to the next bitting depth.

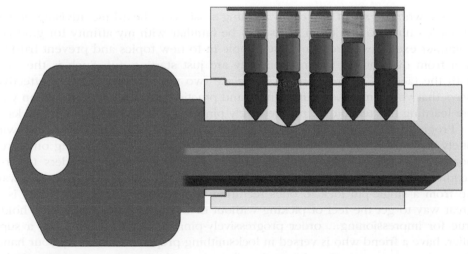

FIGURE 1.91

Now the torpedo pin is hardly binding at all when turning force is applied to the key.

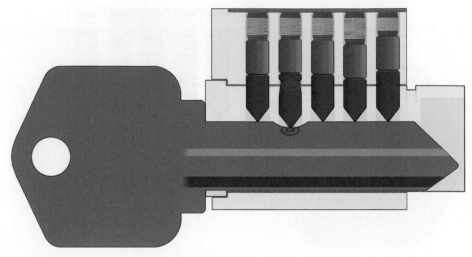

FIGURE 1.92

If the key is wiggled up and down it will barely rub at all against the torpedo pin. Almost no mark will be left, and the person performing the impressioning attack is likely to think that they have found the correct depth and they will probably proceed to another pin position.

TRAINING AIDS AND EXERCISES

Anyone who has sat in one of my training sessions or heard me advising others about learning how to open locks may be familiar with my affinity for gradual, beginner exercises which can ease people in to new topics and prevent frustration from overcoming them when they are just starting out. Such is the case with the tactic of impressioning. There are two very simple and very effective ways that you can make your training and practice go a lot smoother when you are learning this technique: progressively-pinned locks and hard-pinned locks.

Progressive pinning is something that readers of my previous work will likely remember. Instead of having new students attempt lockpicking on store-bought, real-world locks right out of the gate, I encouraged readers to first acquire locks that contained a reduced number of pin stacks. Working their way up from a single-pin lock to ones featuring two and then three pin stacks is a great way to get the feel of picking without diving in headfirst. The same holds true for impressioning… order progressively-pinned training locks from a supplier, have a friend who is versed in locksmithing prepare some, or try your hand at making your own. One interesting fact about the creation of progressively-pinned impressioning training locks: some of the best ones *do not* populate the pin chambers in a predictable order. That is to say, Impression Training Lock Number One should contain only one pin stack, but there is *no need for this pin stack to be in position #1,* right up against the front face of the lock. If the single pin stack in this lock is installed in some random location, deeper within the lock, then part of a user's first lesson is looking at the blade of their key and trying to determine *where* the mark is appearing after they have turned and wiggled the key.

The other useful means of assisting yourself in the initial stages of your impressioning training is to use locks with "hard" pins. By this I am not referring to locks of increased difficulty. Quite the opposite, in fact. I am advocating that you try impressioning on locks that are equipped with pins made of *harder material* than the typically-seen brass. Key pins made of nickel-silver or even stainless steel are sometimes available from locksmithing suppliers. These pins will have a much better likelihood of marking very well against the soft surface of a brass key blank. Once you have tried this a few times, attempt an impressioning attack against a lock with a mix of hard metal pins and traditional brass pins. Over time, you should be able to find and identify impressioning marks left in even the most subtle ways.

All in all, however, perhaps the best thing you can do for yourself when learning to impression is to acquire quality implements. Purchase a sturdy handle which will grip blank keys in a solid manner (a nice pair of Vice-Grips will do at first, but eventually you will want to find a better solution). Set up a nice work space with plenty of light and hopefully a source of magnification (desktop magnifying lamps like the one shown in Figure 1.55 can be found online and in retail stores for $20 or less). Obtain at least one very good file with fine teeth, not from a hardware store but rather from a supplier of locksmithing tools. Get yourself a good supply of **brass** blanks for the locks that you wish to impression; keys made from harder metals are no good and will give beginners a lot of grief when they attempt to mark the keys. Mount a solid vice on a very sturdy table or workbench that isn't going to wiggle all over and you're ready to begin trying this yourself! Good luck!

SUMMARY

This chapter opened with a basic overview of how pin tumbler mechanisms work to ensure that all readers were familiar with the components inside the most common locks in use today. After illustrating just how useful an impressioning attack can be (even when it takes longer to execute than lockpicking), detailed diagrams and step-by-step explanations were given in order to show exactly how this tactic is performed and why it works the way it does. An assortment of tips and advice was offered, in order to assist the reader in understanding how best to see the small marks on the blade of the key and how the key should be filed during an impressioning attack. Popular tools and other hardware were discussed, with examples of commercially-available items as well as home-made equipment that specialists in the lock-opening community have created for themselves. Explanations of impressioning-resistant locks were given, along with advice on how best to proceed when you are attempting this unique tactic for the first time.

I hope that you now see how impressioning can be a very useful tactic for penetration testers. Be creative when you try this in the field. Remember, there is no limit to how much you can choose to distribute this attack. It is possible to pretend that you are using a real key, only to become "distracted" (perhaps by a phone call or conversation with an associate) and walk away in order to inspect the key and perform your filing elsewhere. This can plausibly be done across a period of several days or even weeks, sometimes by different people entirely! While impressioning is rarely the fastest way to open a lock, it has the potential to be one of the most covert methods possible, at least as far as cursory inspection from the outside of the lock is concerned. And remember, once you're in… you're in for good.

Soft Medium Attacks

I hope that this book's substantial opening chapter on the topic of impressioning attacks wasn't too much to present to you all at once. Still, would you agree that the ability to fabricate a working key has the potential to be a much more "powerful" attack in many situations, as opposed to simply *picking* a lock open? The ability to return to a lock on more than one occasion and still open it without the original key (or the ability to operate a lock multiple times in a single session, as is necessary for certain cylinders where the plug must be rotated more than once in order to fully open) is a way to save time and effort that many people consider an attractive prospect.

While use of a file and conventional blank keys may be one of the most reliable ways to produce a fully-functional key which can be used time and again, there are related techniques that often require fewer tools and which can work even more rapidly than "traditional" impressioning attacks. Use of soft mediums or keys coated in malleable materials will sometimes afford you the opportunity to successfully fabricate a rough facsimile of a working key for a lock, and this chapter will discuss some of the most popular tactics in this genre.

Foil keys, wax keys, and mold-and-cast attacks are all lock-opening methods which tend to be grouped rather loosely under the "impressioning" heading, although there is considerable debate among locksmiths and lockpickers as to whether this term is accurate. I usually extend the title of "impressioning" far enough to include the first two techniques mentioned above, but even then I recognize that many people wiser than I might disagree, and thus I favor designating all of these methods under the separate heading of "soft medium" attacks.

FOIL KEYS

The use of thin pieces of metal foil in conjunction with specially-prepared keys can sometimes achieve the same effect as conventional impressioning methods. By applying tension to a lock cylinder, and thus causing pins to bind, it is possible to wiggle a key and cause these binding pins to rub. Unlike with conventional impressioning, however, foil keys do not need to be removed repeatedly from the lock in order to search for rub marks created by the pins. The technician also has no need to shave metal from the key by filing with hand tools. The use of a malleable medium, such as foil, will cause the key to deform at the point where it rubs against a binding pin. Repeated wiggling and oscillating of the key can result in small depressions in the foil or other soft medium, thus allowing the lock to be opened rapidly... sometimes in seconds.

As you will see in this section, the use of foil in attacking a lock can have unpredictable results—and the resultant "keys" are often unstable and not suited for long-term repeated use—but this technique is very effective against certain styles of lock. In particular, locks that operate using *dimple keys* are especially suited to this tactic, for reasons which will be made clear after the concept is explained and demonstrated.

NOTE

It never ceases to amaze me how many names exist for various kinds of hardware. All around the world, certain styles of locks or tools are known by a multitude of surprising designations. In my own experience, flat-profile keys—known most typically in North America as dimple keys—seem to go by a wide variety of names. Invariably, I will attempt to translate the word for "dimple" into the local language of whatever country I'm visiting, then proceed into uncertain territory with local locksmiths, who will eventually understand what I am trying to say (sometimes through my making a quick sketch on paper or by simply pointing to keys in their shop) and then state something to the effect of, "Oh yes, those types of locks are sometimes popular, even if they are a little more expensive. We call them [insert strange name here]."

In parts of the world which often rely on basic, low-cost hardware, I have heard them called simply "security" keys. In parts of the world outside Europe, many people think of them as "Euro" keys, because of that continent's affinity for this design. However you refer to them, these keys do offer some resistance to conventional picking attacks because of the very limited space in the keyway, which makes the use of conventional pick tools difficult. As you will see, however, they are ideal targets for soft-medium attacks.

Figure 2.1 shows a lock and key from LIPS, a Dutch manufacturer that is now part of the ASSA Abloy Group. This formidable lock cylinder features a flat keyway profile and tight machining tolerances. As you can see from the drilled positions on the key, as well as by looking down into the keyway (see Figure 2.2), there are pin stacks contacting the key at all angles, including along its thin edges.

You may have encountered dimple keys at one time or another. Although they may look exotic, internally they are usually just basic pin tumbler mechanisms

FIGURE 2.1

This LIPS lock is a fine example of the "dimple key" design. Holes are drilled into the flat portion of the key blade, accommodating pins which contact the key on its broad sides. On this particular lock, other pin elements also touch the key on its thin edges, although that is less common… most dimple locks simply feature pins that touch the flat portion of the key blade, from either one or both sides. *(Photo courtesy of dosman.)*

FIGURE 2.2

This view, looking down into the keyway of the LIPS lock, shows the pin stacks which are arranged at all angles. *(Photo courtesy of dosman.)*

(see Figures 2.3 and 2.4). They are susceptible to picking attacks (this was discussed in my previous book, *Practical Lock Picking)* either with the use of special-purpose picks or by repurposing typical lockpicking tools.

Dimple locks can also be impressioned in the conventional sense. As seen in Figure 2.5, the insertion of a fully blank key will lift all pin stacks to their maximum position. This will force the driver pins completely out of the plug. At this point, exerting turning pressure on the lock will cause the key pins to bind (see Figure 2.6) and wiggling of the key will cause the key pins to rub and mark (see Figure 2.7). Figure 2.8 shows a photograph of a dimple key in the process of being impressioned.

As can be seen in the photograph in Figure 2.8, the process of conventional impressioning is a bit more difficult and involved when one is working with a dimple lock. The fact that you are not filing into the thin cross-section of a key (as shown in Chapter 1) means removing more metal and creating a cut pattern at odd angles, which can make seeing the impressioning marks difficult... and result in a key that may not function with total precision and smoothness.

However, while dimple locks may not be as suited to file-based impressioning attacks, they are particularly well-matched to tactics which make use of soft mediums... especially foil key attacks.

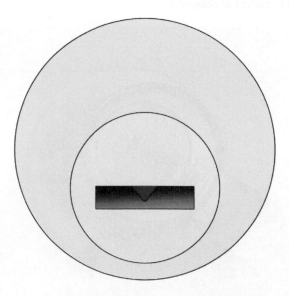

FIGURE 2.3

A dimple lock, as viewed from the outside. The keyway profile may have a "flat" orientation, but you can still see the tip of a conventional tumbler pin within.

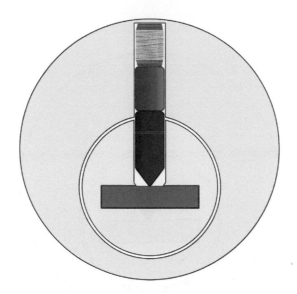

FIGURE 2.5

This diagram represents a blank key being inserted into a dimple lock. The key (represented here simply by a gray rectangle, since we are looking straight at the lock) raises the pin stack high enough such that the drivers (seen in blue) are completely out of the plug.

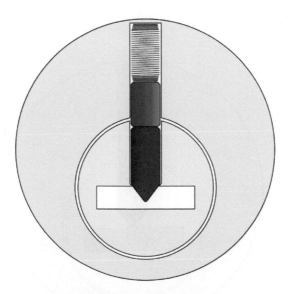

FIGURE 2.4

A dimple lock, shown in a cutaway-view from the same forward-facing perspective as in Figure 2.3. Notice the same manner of pin stack seen in various earlier diagrams. The key pin (shown in red) is lifted by the insertion of a key, and this in turn lifts the driver pin (shown in blue) in order to allow the plug to turn freely. A spring is also a component of this pin stack, much like with conventional "vertically" aligned keys and locks.

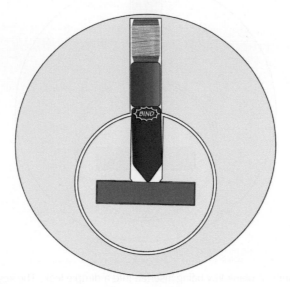

FIGURE 2.6

If an attempt is made to turn the plug of a dimple lock with a blank key, the same effect which was seen in the Chapter 1 will result. The key pins (shown in red) will bind and the lock will not open.

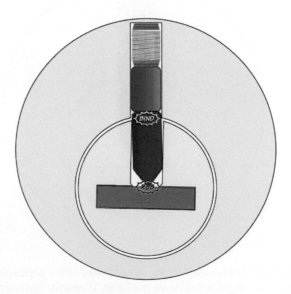

FIGURE 2.7

If a blank key, with turning pressure applied, is wiggled or impacted in some manner, the tip of the key pin will rub against the blade of the blank. This will happen with a dimple key as effectively as with a vertical-style "conventional" key.

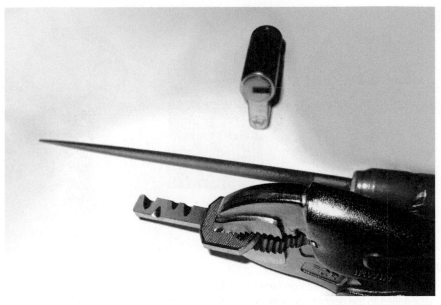

FIGURE 2.8

This is a dimple key blank being shaped and filed during an impressioning attack.

Preparing a foil attack key

In broad strokes, attacks using a foil key mimic the same mechanics of conventional, file-based impressioning in that they involve oscillating the plug and binding certain pins, while slowly "lowering" pin stacks into new positions as you attempt to reach the proper bitting depth in each cut position.

However, unlike conventional impressioning—where a blank key is used—foil impressioning begins with the preparation of a key that has every pin position drilled to the *deepest* possible depth. Figure 2.9 shows such a key.

My good friend dosman, a Co-Founder and member of the Fraternal Order of Locksport, was kind enough to document an outstanding foil-based attack against a LIPS lock. These photographs showcase the remarkable attack that he was able to perform against a high-security lock using very limited supplies and spending little money in the process.

The left side of Figure 2.9 shows the key that was prepared for use during the foil impressioning attack. As this is a two-sided lock, with pins facing the key on multiple surfaces, in some areas the holes prepared on either face of the key blade meet one another and cause perforations directly through the metal. In the middle of Figure 2.9 you can see the piece of aluminum foil that will be used during the attack. The right side of this photograph shows these two components together, with the foil in position on the prepared key.

With the application of a little care and caution, the foil-covered key can be inserted into the lock cylinder (see Figure 2.10).

FIGURE 2.9

Left: a dimple key that has been prepared for a foil-impressioning attack, with each pin position manually drilled to the deepest possible depth. Note how, due to the two-sided nature of this key, in some areas the various holes from either side meet and cause perforations directly through the metal. Center: a piece of aluminum foil to be used during the attack. Right: the prepared key with the foil applied. *(Photo courtesy of dosman.)*

FIGURE 2.10

The foil-covered key has been inserted into the lock. This is one of the hardest parts of performing a foil-based attack... finding a means of inserting the key without the foil becoming fouled in the process. *(Photo courtesy of dosman.)*

Figure 2.11 gives some indication of what is happening within the lock at this stage of the process. A blank key has been prepared by drilling significantly deep holes in each pin position... holes that in many instances should actually be marginally *deeper* than the manufacturer-specified maximum depth. The key has been covered in foil on any faces which will encounter pins. And the key has now fully been inserted into the lock.

TIP

As mentioned in the caption for Figure 2.10, perhaps the most difficult aspect of foil-based attacks is the moment when you are first inserting prepared keys into the victim lock. Since foil is by its very nature an easily bent and easily crinkled medium (that is part of the reason it is used for this technique) it can frequently become fouled when the key is moving past rows of pins. A variety of methods exist to prevent the foil from shifting or crumpling during this moment. Some of the videos on the web site associated with this book even showcase such methods.

Some people will choose to not use bare metal foil, but instead opt to cover their prepared key using foil tape... the type of tape used in the heating and cooling industry. The adhesive backing of such tape helps to prevent the foil from moving out of position on the key. The impressioning attack from the HOPE 2002 conference shown on one of my included videos uses foil tape. Another video I have included, which shows the use of a foil impressioning "kit," incorporates a thin "support rod" which is kept beneath the foil as it is being pushed into the lock. Only after the system has been fully inserted is this rod removed, in order to prevent the force of multiple pins from crushing the foil before the attack begins.

You will no doubt encounter other special methods for protecting the foil before—and even during—attacks like this if you choose to learn more about foil key tactics from other sources.

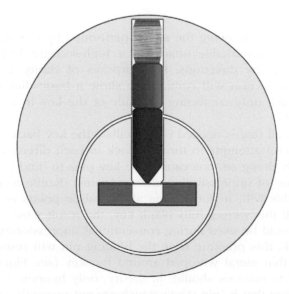

FIGURE 2.11

A key which has been prepared with a deep-drilled hole has been covered in foil and inserted into the lock. This has pushed the pin stack up considerably, much in the same way a blank key would.

FIGURE 2.12

With the foil key in the lock, considerable effort is used while attempting to turn the key in each direction in order to bind the pins and cause small dents in the foil. *(Photo courtesy of dosman.)*

The photographs showing the attack performed by dosman are, of course, documenting his remarkable attack of a high-security lock with pins facing the key in many directions. For purposes of clarity and simplicity, the diagrams in this section will continue to show a basic dimple lock, with the pictured pin stack only contacting one side of the key in a centered position (see Figure 2.11).

At this time, all that is needed is to oscillate the key back and forth, making somewhat forceful attempts to turn the lock in each direction repeatedly (see Figure 2.12). By doing so, one causes the key pins to bind (much as was seen in the discussion of impressioning attacks against dimple locks in Figures 2.6 and 2.7) and this will, in turn, bring about subtle points of pressure against the key itself. If this were a fully blank key, the result would be marks on the metal which would be used during conventional impressioning. However, during a foil attack, this pressure from the binding pin will result in slight deformation of the thin metal wrapped around the key (see Figures 2.13 through 2.15). These deformations should, in theory, only happen beneath pin stacks which are binding that is, pin stacks which are not presently lifted to their ideal height.

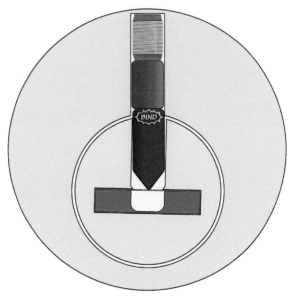

FIGURE 2.13

Binding a pin by attempting to turn the lock while the pin stacks are raised too high.

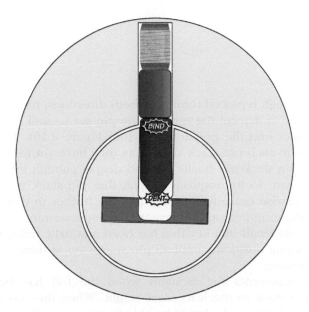

FIGURE 2.14

With a pin binding, the wiggling of the key (which is a natural byproduct of attempting to turn the lock) should cause a small dent in the foil beneath the binding pin.

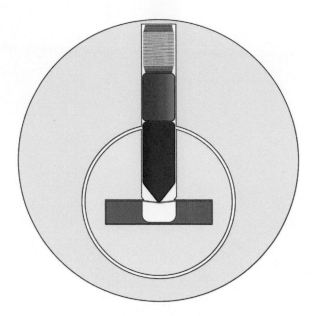

FIGURE 2.15

Even after turning pressure has ceased, the foil should retain the small dent beneath the binding pin in Figure 2.14. The pin stack atop this position is now sitting slightly "lower" than it was before.

Over time, through repeated turning in both directions, the binding and rubbing will continue to deform the foil and the pin stacks will continue to insert deeper and deeper into the prepared key (see Figure 2.16). This should continue happening to each pin stack as long as they have yet to reach their ideal height. When a pin stack has finally pressed deeply enough into the foil that it has "dropped down" to the requisite height, that pin stack will cease to bind and it should likewise cease to dent the foil any further in that spot. Much as was seen with the examination of conventional impressioning in the Chapter 1, this process should result in a key that has been gradually reduced in thickness at the various bitting positions, until all pin stacks are at their ideal height and are no longer binding.

Figure 2.17 represents the moment when the foil has been depressed enough for a pin stack to reach its ideal height. When this has been achieved with *every* pin stack, the lock should be able to turn normally (see Figure 2.18). As you can see in the photograph in Figure 2.19, dosman was able to achieve precisely this exact result with his LIPS lock. Upon removal of the foil key, it is possible to compare it with the original key for the lock and see the relatively parallel markings and depressions shared by each key (see Figure 2.20).

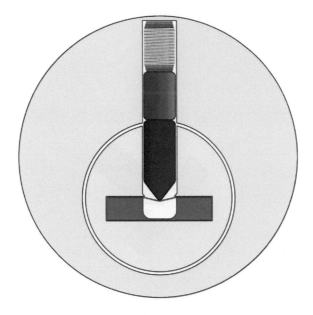

FIGURE 2.16

Subsequent attempts to turn the key in either direction should continue to cause more binding of the pins and thus more denting of the foil. The pin stack should continue to "drop down" further each time.

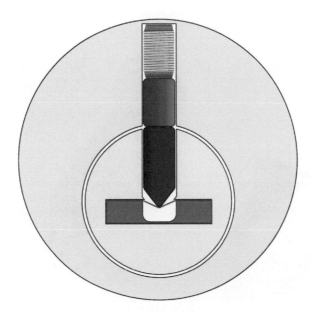

FIGURE 2.17

After repeated turning in either direction, the foil has now become dented to such a degree that—at least in this position—the pin stack has reached its proper height. The pins are no longer binding here, and thus even additional turning should not cause further deformation of the foil.

FIGURE 2.18

When all pins have ceased binding, the process is complete and the lock should turn.

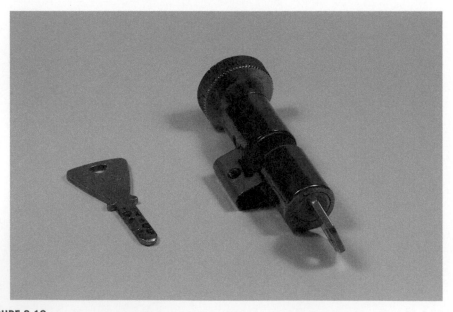

FIGURE 2.19

The foil key attack has been successful. The lock cylinder is now turned and the lock is open. *(Photo courtesy of dosman.)*

FIGURE 2.20

With the key *carefully* removed, it is possible to observe the dents in the foil (both on the broad, flat face of the key as well as along the thin edges) where pins pressed against the key and slowly worked it into the proper shape. *(Photo courtesy of dosman.)*

Now, it is of course highly unlikely that this key which has resulted from a foil impressioning attack would be serviceable for very long. It would be difficult to transport this key unless great care was taken, and the foil key would not usually make for a very useful "original" if a key copying process were attempted. Still, this is an attack that takes very little time to prepare and which can be executed in the field at low cost and with minimal time or noise and no real disturbance to the lock itself... making it quite useful in the right situation.

I suspect that some readers will have noticed that the key in this series of photos showing the foil attack against the LIPS lock was *not* actually prepared using a blank key from this same brand. Although the high-security lock being attacked in these photos is Dutch, the key used was Italian, from the Silca brand. Figure 2.21 shows how similar these keyway profiles are and should convey just how simple it was to turn the blank key of one brand into a foil impressioning base key suitable for attacking another brand of lock.

Foil impressioning kits

Sometimes foil impressioning attacks are performed using specialized hardware. Instead of covering just a deep-drilled *key* with some thin metal sheeting, some lock penetration specialists will make use of kits which can perform foil attacks with greater reliability or which can be used on a wide range of locks. After all, aside from situations like the one shown in Figure 2.21 (where one brand of key could be used in a different brand of lock), usually a key-based foil attack will only work if you have access to the appropriate blank keys for a given lock. Specialized foil-impressioning kits, however, can be designed with some degree of universality in mind and thus will give their owner the means to attack a wider range of locks without the need to possess a great number of blank keys.

A video on this book's web site features Raf, a TOOOL member showcasing a foil impressioning kit which he has found to be highly effective against dimple locks in parts of Europe. This kit features a faux-key into which prepared segments of foil can be inserted, and the whole affair is operated by means of a large handle (see Figure 2.22). As the video demonstrates, this tool is quite effective in the right hands (see Figure 2.23) and the results are nearly identical to what was observed in the previous photographs of the attack against the LIPS lock (see Figure 2.24). The foil impressioning kit featured in this video is available here… http://www.lockpick.me/05-chanpin/p-001-1.asp?id=1913.

FIGURE 2.21

Left: The Dutch LIPS brand key which was originally issued with the lock seen in previous photos. Center: A key blanks for the Italian Silca brand of locks. Right: A Silca brand key blank which has been drilled in the LIPS pin positions and had its tip re-shaped, in order to be used as a base key for a foil impressioning attack against a LIPS lock. *(Photo courtesy of dosman.)*

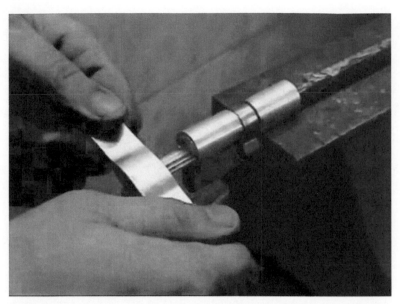

FIGURE 2.22

A still frame from video footage of Raf using his foil impressioning kit. This is the moment when the device is being inserted into the lock to be attacked.

FIGURE 2.23

A still frame from video footage of Raf using his foil impressioning kit. The lock has been opened and is turning freely.

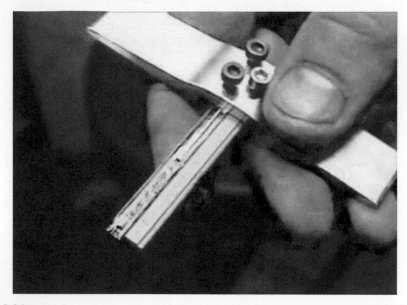

FIGURE 2.24

A still frame from video footage of Raf using his foil impressioning kit. Once removed from the lock, the foil can be seen with dents in the positions where pins were pressing.

When foil fails

As useful as many of these techniques are, users of foil key tactics do occasionally encounter difficulty when working with these thin, temperamental materials. Certain key profiles will behave very differently from others.

All of the examples in this section of the chapter have tended to focus on dimple style locks because they are the most suited to the use of foil on specially-prepared keys. Dimple-style bitting holes drilled into keys will tend to support the foil material from all sides and all angles… it is roughly akin to draping a gardening tarp over a hole dug into soil. If the soil is firm (and perhaps if the edges of the tarp are weighted somewhat) the area over top of the hole should be able to maintain its shape and even support a small load with relative ease.

Contrast this hypothetical scenario with a different situation… one in which that same plastic tarp is draped over a series of bare fence posts sticking out of the ground. How well will the tarp maintain its shape in this situation? Will winds or debris thrown against it cause it to bend or buckle? They most likely will. Would you consider trying to lay any objects upon the tarp along its top-facing, folded edge? More than likely, this would just result in the whole affair wrinkling and caving in further… it would possibly even rip or tear. It is for this reason that most security professionals dislike attempting foil-based attacks against "traditional" pin tumbler locks in which the key is held "vertically" and the pins only contacts them along the thin edge of the key blade.

This type of tactic does exist, however. Use of a specially-prepared key featuring deep, wide grooves cut into the blade is required. Seen in Figure 2.25, this type of key is sometimes referred to as a "comb"-style key, although I dislike this term given that other (entirely unrelated) tools exist which are known as comb picks. (Use of those tools was discussed in my previous book, *Practical Lock Picking*.) When attempting a foil-based attack against this manner of lock, the foil piece is draped over this prepared key (see Figure 2.26) and pressed flush against the blade. If the foil being used has any adhesive backing, this will help it cling and stay in place securely (see Figure 2.27).

With great care, one then attempts to insert the foil-wrapped key into the lock, thus raising all of the pins to their maximum height (see Figure 2.28). A

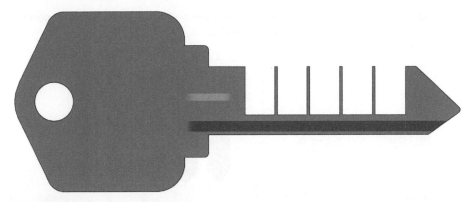

FIGURE 2.25

This is the style of "key" used during a foil-impressioning attack of a vertical keyway lock. There's really not a lot of metal there to support the foil, and damage to these keys is common during the impressioning process.

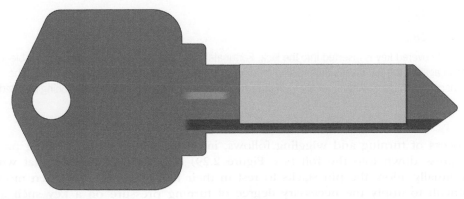

FIGURE 2.26

Foil is draped over the blade of the specially-prepared key.

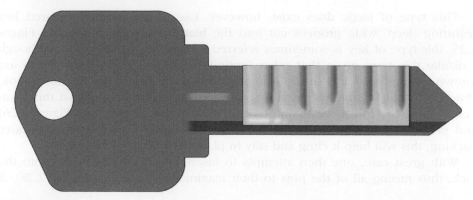

FIGURE 2.27

The foil is pressed into place. If the foil sheet has an adhesive backing, this will help to secure it and prevent the foil from slipping as the key is inserted.

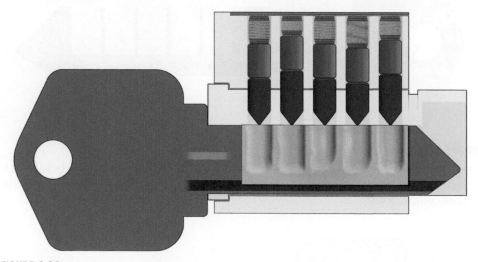

FIGURE 2.28

The foil-covered key is inserted into the lock. Fortunately, the original metal tip of the key is able to ride in against the pin stacks first, raising them up and working against the spring pressure. The foil need only have enough integrity to *maintain* the pins at this height as the key is being inserted.

process of turning and wiggling follows, in an attempt to cause binding pins to press down into the foil (see Figure 2.29) causing deformations that will eventually allow the pin stacks to rest in their ideal heights. It is often more difficult to apply the necessary degree of turning pressure on a key such as this, given how much of the blade is missing. Sometimes, if there is room in the keyway, a tension tool or other implement is simultaneously inserted into

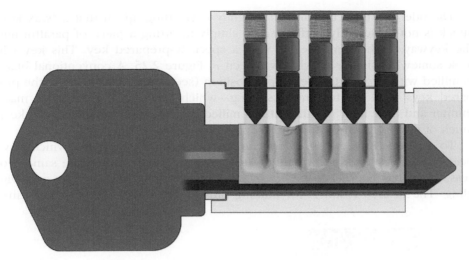

FIGURE 2.29

The idea with foil impressioning is to create dents in the soft, thin metal sheet whenever pins are binding. Sometimes this works, but very often it does not. I've never encountered an especially reliable and robust foil-impressioning kit for use in vertical-keyway locks.

the plug to provide additional turning pressure without causing harm to the key. This method of using an auxiliary tool actually can be seen in one of the foil-impressioning videos available on the web site associated with this book. It is not a vertical-keyway lock being attacked in that video, but the dimple key being featured is thin enough and the pins are contacting so close to the edge of the key that the tactician shown has chosen to use an additional tool in order to provide extra tension without damaging the key.

I have performed foil-impressioning techniques a number of times. However, even under controlled conditions with professional equipment, I have never seen very effective and quick results when working on a lock with a *vertical* keyway. In my experience, it is much better to approach situations like that by using conventional impressioning tactics (filing or cutting a key in stages). However, if you truly want to try using a soft medium on most of the locks in North America… there's always wax.

WAX KEYS

The previous section discussed how foil-wrapped keys can be used to perform an impressioning attack, in a manner of speaking. It also described how this tactic tends to fare much better against dimple locks as opposed to vertical-blade-style mechanisms. There are some people who choose to use soft mediums to attack more "traditional" vertical keyway locks, however… and often, the malleable material they choose to use in these locks is wax.

The title of this section may be slightly misleading, given that a "wax key" attack is not exclusively performed by simply inserting a piece of paraffin into the keyway. Rather, one begins with a specially-prepared key. This key will look somewhat similar to what was seen in Figure 2.25. A conventional blank is milled with deep cuts in each pin position (see Figure 2.30). Unlike the prepared keys used for foil impressioning—which often have their sides made thinner and have their profile features milled down—wax attack keys can keep much of their original profile and shape on the sides.

To use this key, wads of wax are inserted in the hollows which have been created by the special milling (see Figure 2.31) and then the same process which has been seen before is attempted: turning and binding and wiggling. The desired result is for binding pins to press into the wax and cause

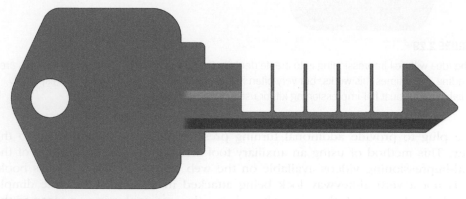

FIGURE 2.30

A key prepared for use with a wax impressioning tactic. It looks quite similar to a key used for foil impressioning.

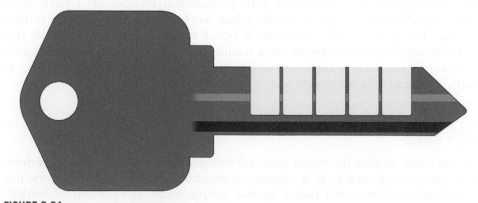

FIGURE 2.31

The wax key is now ready for use.

deformations (see Figure 2.32) until they reach the ideal depth. If each pin stack can be made to no longer bind, the lock will turn. Getting the key back out again, however... that is sometimes a tricky prospect!

Wax-filled keys can also be used to impression other styles of locks, as well. Dimple locks—which were shown earlier in the discussion of foil impressioning— have been subject to these same attacks for some time now.

To prepare a wax-impressioning key for a dimple lock, a blank key is needed (see Figure 2.33) which will fit easily in the keyway. This key is then

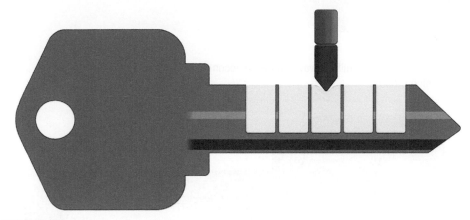

FIGURE 2.32

Unlike the tactic discussed directly above, where foil is draped over a vertically-held key blade, wax impressioning should usually proceed in such a way that dents in one part of the key do not affect the soft medium in other areas.

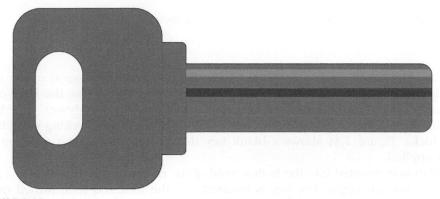

FIGURE 2.33

A blank key for a dimple lock. This key will be used in these examples to showcase wax impressioning in a horizontal, flat-profile keyway.

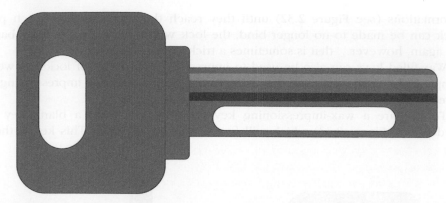

FIGURE 2.34

A large area of the key is milled away in order to accommodate the use of wax for the impressioning process.

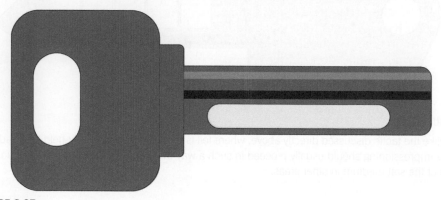

FIGURE 2.35

With wax in the hollow area of the prepared key, the impressioning process can proceed.

typically milled in a way that removes all materials from the region of the key blade which would normally contact the pins during use. Unlike the keys prepared for wax impressioning of vertical-keyway locks (seen above), it is less common to mill each pin position individually when you are working with dimple locks. Figure 2.34 shows a blank key that is ready to have a segment of wax applied.

With wax inserted into the hollow void of the prepared key (see Figure 2.35) the process can begin. The key is inserted into the lock and then turned from side to side repeatedly, in an attempt to get the pin stacks to bind and cause dents in the soft medium. The process is almost identical to the foil-impressioning of dimple keys which was described earlier in this chapter.

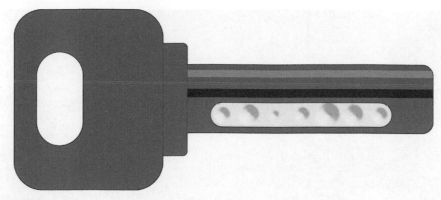

FIGURE 2.36

If successful, the resultant wax impressioned key should look something like this. While it is not usually suitable for use in a key duplication machine (and, indeed, this key may not even survive repeated insertion back into the lock) it could conceivably be measured with a depth gauge and used to decode the proper bitting for this lock.

If you are successful, the result should be a key with dents in the wax which represent the ideal cut depths in each pin position (see Figure 2.36). It is usually somewhat easier to remove a wax-impressioned key from a flat dimple keyway than a conventional vertically-aligned keyway. This tends to be due to the fact that pins don't stick as deeply into a dimple key as they do into a vertically-aligned key blade.

MOLD-AND-CAST ATTACKS

One other technique of opening locks involves covertly copying a legitimate key by making a cast of it in a soft medium, then using this imprint to fabricate a working key at a later time. While this process does involve making an "impression" of sorts (when the original key is pressed into the soft material) most locksmiths and lockpickers would agree that the term *impressioning* does not apply to this technique. Most properly referred to as a mold-and-cast attack, the idea of quickly copying a key which one may have access to for only a few moments is by no means a modern development.

The first time I saw this technique, I was seated in a movie theater. My family and I were viewing the film *The First Great Train Robbery*, a masterful work which presents a fictionalized retelling of the Great Gold Robbery of 1855, which was an actual historic event that involved a number of physical security and social engineering attacks... many of which are portrayed in the film. A number of key points in the movie's plot surround the lead characters (portrayed by Sean Connery and Donald Sutherland) and their attempts to

FIGURE 2.37

In the film *The First Great Train Robbery*, we see Robert Agar (portrayed by Donald Sutherland) attempting to pick open a locked door while his associate, Edward Pierce (portrayed by Sean Connery) acts as lookout.

find and duplicate the keys to high-security safe locks which protect shipments of gold. In the film—which also prominently features conventional lockpicking on occasion (see Figure 2.37)—Sutherland's character, a safe-cracker and thief named Robert Agar, uses a wax impressioning kit to make copies of the Chubb safe keys needed for the robbery (see Figures 2.38 through 2.44).

The film was very true to the methods and technology available at this time in history. During the mid-nineteenth century, mold-and-cast tactics of key copying were often used as a means of quickly creating a *record* of the original key. The wax imprint was rarely used *directly* in the fabrication of additional keys. A skilled locksmith or safe technician would manually file and craft a working key, comparing it frequently with the details left in the wax.

Some modern key-copying kits work in this same manner. Wax is not the most typical medium anymore, having been replaced to some degree by clays and synthetic putty compounds. Also, modern machining techniques have produced "clamshell" style cases, which feature soft material in lids on each side, allowing a key to be briefly enclosed while an impression is made of each face at the same time. Much as was the case over a century ago, however, these tools are often used to simply make rapid *recordings* of keys. The actual creation of a *duplicate* key takes place later, often with the aid of measuring tools and/or a code-cutting machine.

FIGURE 2.38

Pierce (Connery) has found the key which he and Robert Agar (Sutherland) are seeking. It is now up to his partner to make an impression of the key in wax.

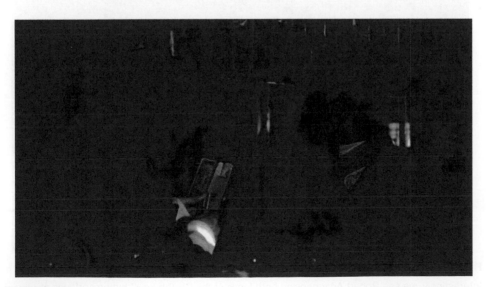

FIGURE 2.39

Agar (Sutherland) is seen pressing the Chubb key into a block of wax kept in a small tin.

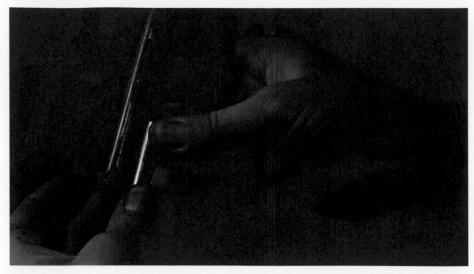

FIGURE 2.40

Agar is pressing the key into the wax in order to record the details of its bitting cuts.

FIGURE 2.41

Interestingly, we see Robert Agar copying both faces of the Chubb keys' bitting surfaces at various points during *The First Great Train Robbery*... but I can think of few situations when these two surfaces would ever offer different information.

FIGURE 2.42

The thin edge of the bitting surface as well as the front profile of the Chubb key is also pressed into the wax. Agar's work is now complete, and he shows the results to Pierce.

FIGURE 2.43

A wax impression of a key can act as a useful *guide* regarding the bitting depths and cut positions of the real key, but the wax itself is rarely used in the fabrication of a working key. This process is performed by hand, in a meticulous and step-by-step manner.

FIGURE 2.44

The results of Robert Agar's work... a functioning key for one of the many Chubb safes which the stars of the film seek to open during their gold heist.

Lately, an interesting new line of soft-medium products has begun to emerge, however. Making use of modern polymer compounds and metals with low melting points, these systems can truly be called *key-duplicating* kits, as opposed to mechanisms which are used solely for documenting the shape of a key. Among the best of these kits which I have evaluated is the Quick Key system. Made in Germany, this package uses a binary medium in which to cast an image of the target key. These materials are soft and malleable in their natural state, but once combined they quickly harden and form a very resilient record of anything pressed against them during the curing process. The Quick Key package also relies on rods of specially-blended metal (my associates and I suspect that bismuth plays a significant role in their composition) which will melt easily and rapidly and can be used to form a working key almost immediately, right there in the field.

Because of the extreme usefulness of this package (and also due to the almost complete lack of any included instructions or guide information online) the remainder of this chapter will describe, step-by-step, the process for using the Quick Key system.

Quick Key copying

The Quick Key kit comes with the components seen in Figure 2.45. Two containers of composite compound (enough to use the kit between eight and ten times, I'd estimate), a rod of low-melting-point metal, a heating cup, and a two-piece milled tray system complete the package. In order to use the kit in the field, one should also source the items shown in Figure 2.46. A micro-torch, a small clamp or gripper, and an X-Acto style knife are all almost essential to the process.

FIGURE 2.45

The Quick Key system consists of these items: binary molding compound, metal stock, a heating cup, and a two-piece aluminum tray.

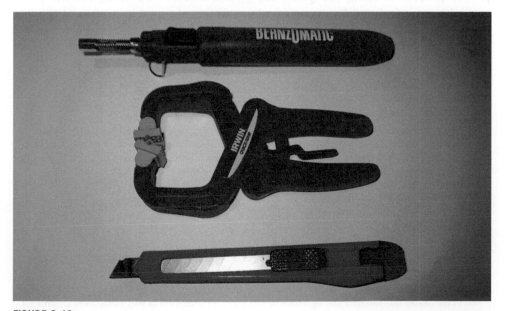

FIGURE 2.46

To use the Quick Key system, it is almost essential that you have at your disposal a butane micro-torch, a clamp or Vice-Grip, and a small blade.

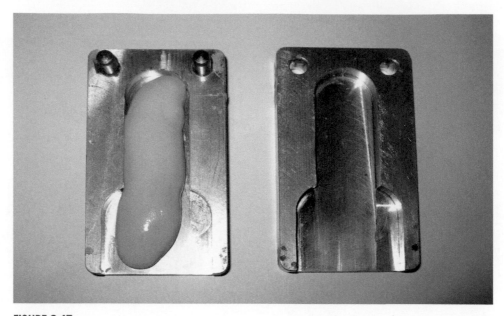

FIGURE 2.47

One half of the binary compound is prepared, by filling one of the two pieces of the casting trays.

The process of using the Quick Key system will involve filling the two-piece tray with a wad of molding compound consisting of equal measures of the two materials supplied in small plastic jars. An easy way to prepare the necessary amount of these two materials is to fill each side of the tray separately (see Figures 2.47 through 2.50).

WARNING

The two materials which form the binary compound are very sensitive to one another. Any exposure at all, even from residue left on your hands (as can be seen in Figure 2.48) will invariably start the chemical reaction and begin hardening the materials if cross-contamination happens. Be sure to take precautions to avoid *any* mixing of these two materials until the exact moment you are preparing to copy a key.

Wash your hands in between moments when you are touching either compound. And, most of all, never reach into one jar if you have just handled material from the other. It is possible to spoil an entire supply of this material if you are not careful.

TIP

On penetration testing jobs, some people will choose to keep their Quick Key kit at the ready by filling each side of the casting tray and then placing a sheet of wax paper between them as they clamp them together for transport in a pocket or backpack. This is an acceptable short-term solution, but I do not recommend this for long term storage or transport for more than a few hours.

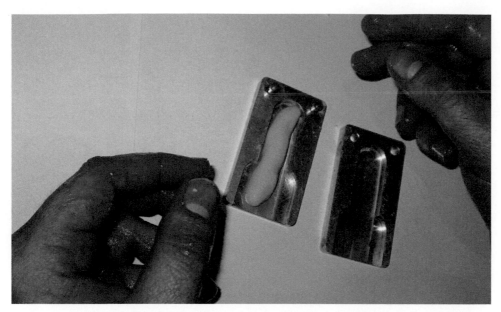

FIGURE 2.48

These compounds will often leave residue on your hands... be careful to wash it off before you touch the other binary medium; otherwise, you may start the hardening reaction before you are ready to do so!

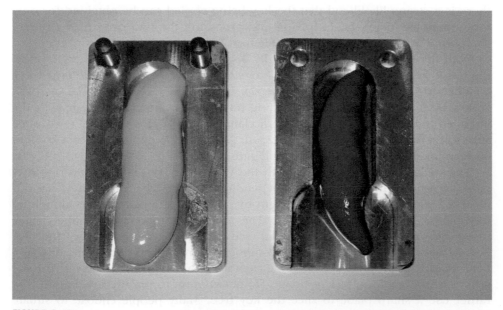

FIGURE 2.49

Both sides of the casting tray are now seen with an allotment of the binary compound.

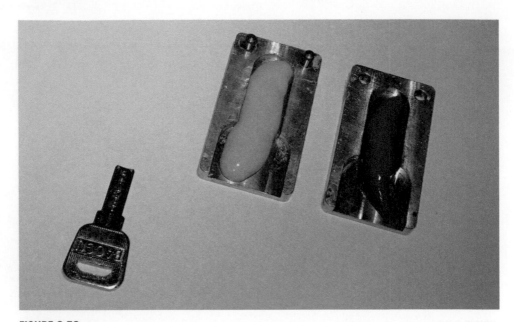

FIGURE 2.50

This key is about to be copied using the Quick Key system.

When the time has come to copy a key (in these situations it is assumed that there is a strong likelihood that the key being copied can be obtained for only a few minutes' time), begin mixing and preparing the two parts of the binary compound in the manner shown in Figures 2.51 through 2.56.

With the molding compound rapidly beginning to harden, it is time to insert the target key and affix the two trays together tightly. Simply *lay* the target key on one side of the kit (see Figure 2.57). Do not use excessive force or mash it down deeply. Place the other casting tray into position, aligning it with the included pins and holes, and use your clamp or Vice-Grips to apply even pressure to the whole affair (see Figure 2.58). Allow the compound at least another 60 seconds to fully set and cure (see Figure 2.59).

The trickiest part of working with the Quick Key system is when one prepares to remove the original key. Depending on the shape of the key, various levels of effort will be involved. Begin by gently separating the two aluminum tray pieces, as seen in Figure 2.60. The molding compound will likely have fused into one solid block of material (see Figure 2.61). This stage of the process is the most difficult. When the compound hardens, it retains a slightly rubbery feeling, but it does not have the capability to bend easily. Too much force will cause the mold to tear or break. Do not attempt to pry the mold apart, but rather use a sharp blade to slice the key free. Many people choose to situate the block of compound back into one of the trays in order to assist in this process (see Figure 2.62). Once the mold is separated and the key has been safely removed, all that will remain is the imprint of the bitting and profile contours,

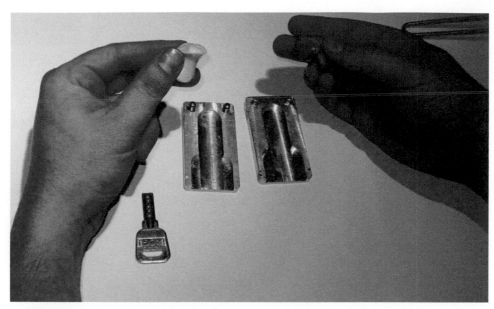

FIGURE 2.51

Remove the two halves of the binary compound from their respective trays.

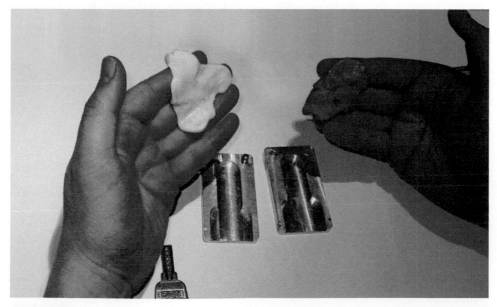

FIGURE 2.52

Begin by squashing each bit of compound rather flat in your hands.

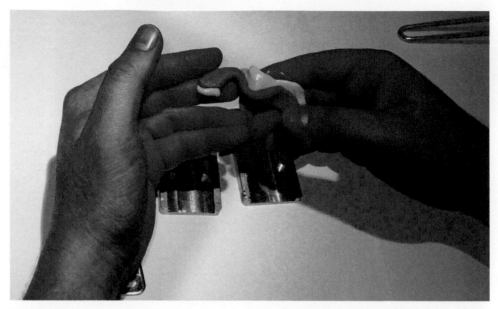

FIGURE 2.53

Mash the two parts together, exposing as much of their surface area as you can. Once they have started to combine, you will have approximately 30 to 40 seconds maximum before hardening begins.

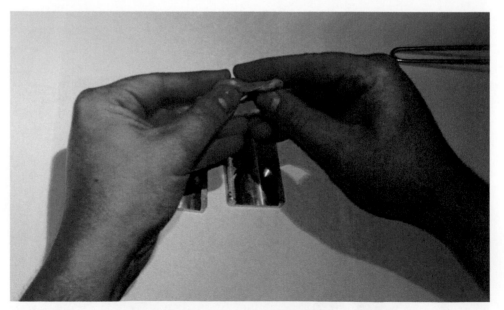

FIGURE 2.54

Knead and fold the mass of compound as quickly as you can. If you begin to feel its temperature rising, that is a sign that the chemical reaction is proceeding.

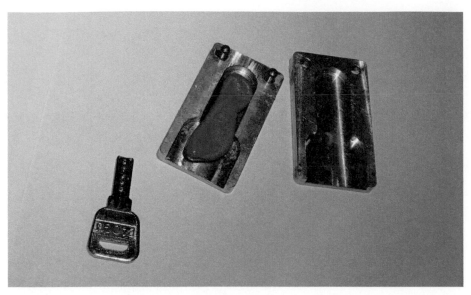

FIGURE 2.55

After about 30 seconds of kneading and mixing with your hands, separate the mass of compound into two equal parts. You will have to use the 10 seconds or so that remain before hardness sets in to spread these two separate masses into the trays.

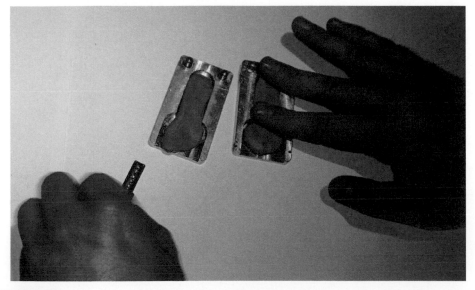

FIGURE 2.56

Do not worry about filling out the entire tray perfectly on either side. Just get the compound spread somewhat evenly and without pressing too deeply with your fingers. The Quick Key compound should be more or less flush with the lip of the casting tray on each side.

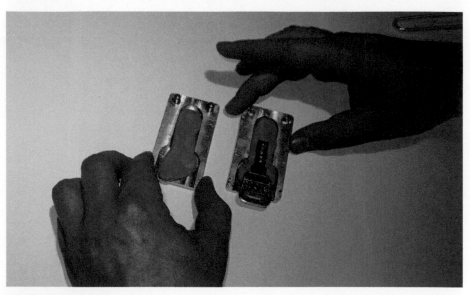

FIGURE 2.57

When you are positioning your key to be copied, do not press it down hard into the molding compound. Simply lay it upon the material in one tray. It will become adequately compressed from both sides during the next step.

FIGURE 2.58

Working fast because of the rapidly-setting compound, position the two aluminum trays together and clamp the whole affair together tightly. It's alright if the key skews or is off-center slightly… what matters most is that the molding compound is making good contact with both sides of the original key.

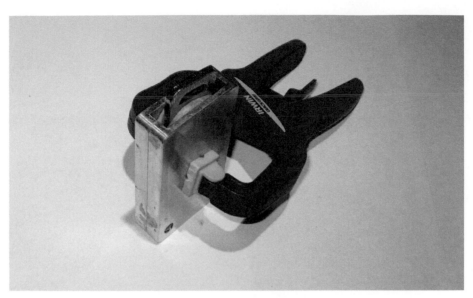

FIGURE 2.59

With the trays clamped together, give the compound at least one minute to cure and harden completely. You can check whether it has set or not by poking at the exposed material with the tip of a lockpick or a fingernail.

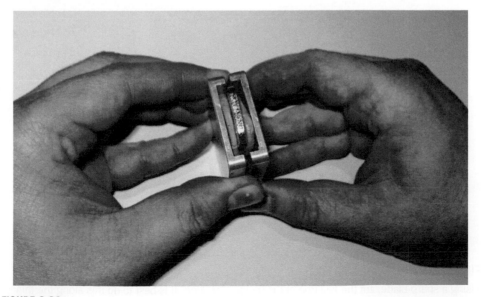

FIGURE 2.60

The process of removing the original key from the mold compound is a delicate one. Begin by slowly separating the two aluminum trays.

FIGURE 2.61

After it has cured and hardened, the mold compound will be more or less one solid mass. It will have to be gently and carefully cut apart.

FIGURE 2.62

Using a sharp blade, cut the key free of the mold compound. It is best to do this along the thin edge of the key. Many people find it helpful to situate the block of solid mold compound in one (or both) of the aluminum trays while doing so.

FIGURE 2.63

With the key carefully removed (and ostensibly returned to its proper place after what has been only a very brief absence) the mold now bears the exact shape needed to create a new key.

as seen in Figure 2.63. Reassemble the two aluminum trays and the mold compound, using your clamp to keep the whole package upright, as you prepare to create the replacement key (see Figure 2.64).

The Quick Key kit comes with a small metal heating cup. Ignite your micro torch and begin warming this cup as shown in Figure 2.65. In about 30 seconds, you will be ready to begin melting some of your source metal. Touch the bar of metal stock included in the Quick Key kit to the inner edge of the heating cup. It should almost immediately begin to liquefy (see Figure 2.66).

WARNING

As you heat the source bar, a small amount of smoke and vapor is typically released. While we have not investigated the specific metal blend that is used to create the Quick Key bar stock, many users (including this author) have reported unpleasant effects related to any inhalation of this smoke. Be certain to work in a well-ventilated area and take care to avoid breathing the fumes created when the metal melts.

It is difficult to know exactly how much metal will be needed when making a replacement key, but I find it is best to err on the side of caution. Be conservative with your estimates. After all, you can always melt a little more bar stock if the key you produce is too small. Once you have enough liquid metal in your

FIGURE 2.64

The whole kit, including the newly-created mold, is prepared for the casting of a new key.

FIGURE 2.65

A micro torch is best for heating the metal included in the Quick Key kit.

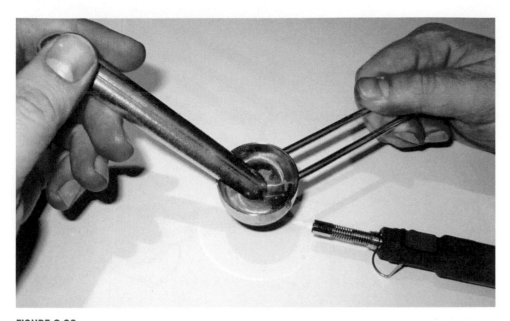

FIGURE 2.66

The metal should begin to liquefy almost immediately upon touching the preheated cup.

heating cup such that the surface area looks to be slightly larger than the size of a nickel, you are likely ready to create your key (see Figure 2.67).

TIP

Take care to not "over cook" your metal once it has reached its liquid state. Not only will this likely produce even more smoke and fumes of the sort discussed in the warning above, but excessive heating also tends to interfere with how the metal will behave, leading to difficulty in casting and the production of weaker keys.

Bring the heating cup over to the casting mold which should still be clamped and waiting in a vertical position. Pour the entire contents of the cup into the mold (see Figure 2.68). Do not worry about any excess or runoff. It will harden quickly and can be cleaned up with relative ease, as long as you are working on a hard surface.

The creators of the Quick Key system recommend rapidly tapping the mold on the surface of your work area as soon as the pour is completed, in order to ensure that the metal flows into all small cracks and crevices. I personally do not know how much this can accomplish, as the metal will begin hardening quickly... although despite my being skeptical, I tend to follow this advice every time. Wait at least one minute for the metal to harden and cool before you attempt to remove it from the mold. In truth, 60 seconds is the *absolute minimum* time one should pause at this stage of the process. If you are working with

FIGURE 2.67

The metal in the cup is fully liquefied and ready to be turned into a new key.

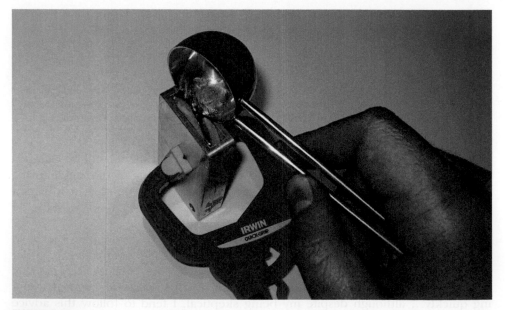

FIGURE 2.68

Pouring the liquid metal into the mold in order to cast a new key can be tricky, but after one or two attempts you'll find it relatively straightforward. If you make any mistakes, you can always clean up spilled metal once it cools and then melt it again for use in subsequent attempts.

a particularly delicate or thin style of key, it is not a bad idea to double or even triple this delay as you give the metal time to fully harden.

NOTE

My use of the word "harden" may be slightly amiss, since the metal used in the Quick Key system will *never* become as hard and stiff as steel or even brass. You should not expect the resultant keys to perform in the manner that conventional keys can. Treat them carefully and *never* force them if they do not insert or turn with ease in a lock.

After you have waited for the metal to cool and harden, separate the two aluminum trays and peel the mold compound apart (see Figure 2.69). This should be considerably easier than the first time you did this. You will not likely require a blade. You should now have a newly-created key that very closely parallels the shape and size of the original, as seen in Figure 2.70.

Try to operate the lock using this new key. If the key does not insert or the plug does not want to turn *do not attempt to force it.* Remove the key and examine it closely. Give close scrutiny to edges, particularly where the two

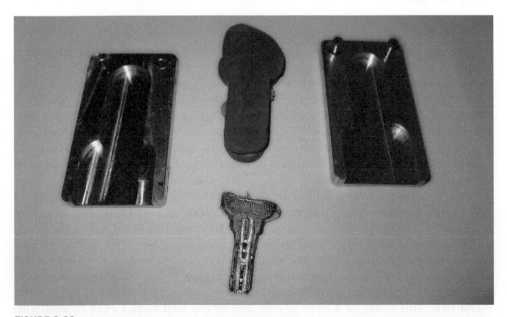

FIGURE 2.69

With the mold separated, the key can be carefully removed. It should be hard enough to handle and inspect, but do take care to not damage it... it is not as strong as a conventional key made of brass, nickel, or steel!

FIGURE 2.70

If you have been successful in your use of the Quick Key kit, the resultant key should be rather true to the original.

halves of the molding compound came together. It is typical for imperfect "seams" in the mold to result in a little excess material on the key in these areas, especially at the very tip of the key. Much as Donald Sutherland's character had to tweak and adjust the final details of his copied keys in *The First Great Train Robbery*, it may be necessary for you to perfect any keys which you create using the Quick Key mold-and-cast kit. Careful use of a hand file or emery board can remove some of the excess metal, and careful jiggling and cajoling of the key within the lock will usually result in everything working in the end (see Figure 2.71).

You can save the two halves of your mold compound once it is hard, in order to re-use them to create more keys as often as you wish. The key seen in Figure 2.72 was at least the third or fourth copy produced using the same mold. Exposure to the hot metal does not degrade or erode the rubbery compound in any significant way. The metal itself is also re-usable. Keys which are no longer needed can be easily melted down (see Figure 2.73) and converted into small, round pellets which can be used on future occasions. I used the metal from this example key to re-cast one of the first keys I ever copied with the Quick Key system. I still had the mold I created years ago for the ASSA Desmo key seen in Figure 2.74, and I was easily able to fabricate a duplicate copy yet again.

FIGURE 2.71

It may take some jiggling and tweaking, but in the end these rapidly-created keys will usually operate a lock without much difficulty. Remember, you should not have to apply considerable effort when using these keys! Do not force them, as they can easily be bent or broken.

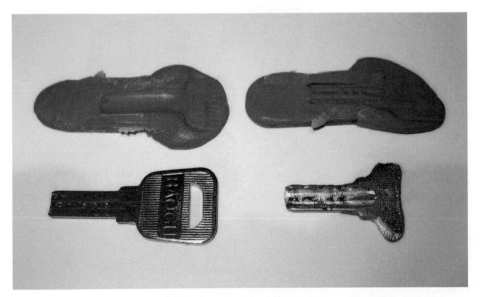

FIGURE 2.72

Repeated casting of hot metal does not damage the mold compound. I used this same mold four times in the creation of these photos, with no ill effects on the keys being produced.

FIGURE 2.73

Old keys created with the Quick Key system can be melted down and the metal can be easily reused later.

FIGURE 2.74

I found a mold I had created years ago for an ASSA Desmo key, and it still worked perfectly. Using the metal from this example session, I was able to re-create a copy of the ASSA key as if I had access to the original years later. (That *is* the original key, actually, in the lower front portion of this photograph. The copy created using the Quick Key kit appears above it.)

SUMMARY

This chapter explored a number of ways that soft mediums can be employed in the creation of working keys for locks you wish to open. Sometimes these are materials like foil or wax applied directly to a key, in order to rapidly (albeit sometimes imperfectly) attempt an impressioning-style process. Other times, soft compounds can be used to a make a mold of a working key in order to duplicate it at a later time.

All in all, most attacks using soft materials drive a middle-of-the-road path which seeks to strike a balance between the opposing aspects of speed and reliability. Most soft key attacks can be executed more rapidly than procedures like impressioning with a file or manipulation with lockpicks, but the results tend to be slightly unpredictable and many times the resultant "open" status of the lock is not easily repeated.

While it is unlikely that any penetration specialist will come to rely on soft-material tools 100 percent of the time, they can become a useful part of a larger arsenal of equipment carried on jobs. Practice some of these techniques, enough so that you know what to expect when attempting the tactics described here, and perhaps you will encounter a situation where a soft medium will play a useful role in opening a lock which you are unable to quickly and effectively defeat by other means.

Master-Keyed Systems

CHAPTER OUTLINE

INTRODUCTION

Most residential locks and virtually *all* locks purchased at local hardware stores are designed to operate with a single key. That is, only one particular *bitting* (or combination of cuts on the blade of the key) will allow the plug to turn and cause the lock to open. If you wish to endow additional people with the ability to enter a door when it is equipped with such a simple lock, you simply make a copy of the key. If you have multiple doors on a single building and they are all operated by this key, you are effectively granting new users *total* access every time another copy is made. Naturally, this is not ideal for many commercial settings.

Many businesses, schools, and other large institutions wish to maintain tighter controls regarding which users have the ability to open which doors. Some people—students or faculty, for example—may be authorized to enter their particular building or their personal office only. Other people—such as maintenance personnel—might have access to all of the rooms on a specific building but are barred from entering different rooms elsewhere on campus. And, of course, some people—such as security guards or upper management types—will have permission to go anywhere that they wish. Sometimes, these privileges are bestowed simply in the form of additional keys... in these situations, those with the most access rights also tend to have the most brass dangling and jingling from their belt. In the interest of reducing the number of keys that people are forced to carry in order to do their jobs, many larger facilities are *master-keyed*.

Master-keying is the configuration of a system of locks in such a way that certain keys have more rights and privileges than others. A large number of the readers of this book may have interacted with master-keyed lock systems at one time or another, even if they did not know it at the time. These systems are relatively simple (at least from a mechanical perspective) and are widely-deployed, particularly in commercial and educational environments.

Master-keyed systems make the logistics of granting access somewhat simpler—they also make things simpler for each end user, since fewer keys need to be carried by each person—but they can also weaken an organization's overall security. Not only does it tend to be easier to pick or to impression master-keyed locks (simply because of the increased number of shear lines across all of the pin stacks) but master-keyed systems also tend to leak information in a number of ways. Dedicated attackers who have the ability to spend a bit of time will often have the ability to compromise the code for the top master key (with the most access privileges) in nearly all master-keyed systems, given only minor preliminary information and a small number of blank keys.

NOTE

Before we embark on this exploration of master-keyed systems and how to attack them, we must acknowledge the exceptional research and reporting performed in this field by Matt Blaze. A professor at the University of Pennsylvania (and before that a researcher and engineer at AT&T Labs) Blaze has had a long-standing love affair with all things related to security, cryptology, and privacy. Included in his passion are the topics of locks and lockpicking.

In 2003, Blaze published a famous paper in the journal *Security and Privacy* which detailed vulnerabilities in master-keyed systems. Most of the details in his piece, *Rights Amplification in Master-Keyed Mechanical Locks,* were already known in private circles (among locksmiths and the like) but this was the first time the research and engineering communities—indeed, the members of the public as a whole—were fully exposed to the weight of these facts.

All of us in the lockpicking and physical security communities owe a debt of gratitude to Matt Blaze and all other researchers like him, who choose to responsibly disclose vulnerabilities when they are discovered. By teaching others, we improve security for ourselves and for one another. Better products may be introduced and existing policies may be amended… but only if people speak out and discuss the problems which they find. I hope that this process continues, and that engineers, academics, and even the hobbyist lockpicking community continues to share information and work toward better security for everyone, one lock at a time.

WARNING

Please be aware, this text book is *not* a locksmith training manual, nor is it a locksmithing reference guide. The intricacies of designing, deploying, and maintaining a master-keyed system far exceed what can easily be covered in a single chapter such as this. This section of the book should give most people sufficient awareness of the workings of master-keyed systems so that they are able to understand how they function and how to potentially attack them, but I could not begin to hope to cover all of the manifold details of how such systems can be arranged and configured.

If you are considering a career in locksmithing, you will need to have a firm grasp of many details before you should attempt to address customer needs. If you are embarking on the development of a master-keyed system, you would do well to have a full understanding of terms and abbreviations such as Total Position

Progression (TPP), Rotating Constant (RC), and Maximum Adjacent Cut Specification (MACS). This book will sometimes make passing references to these and other technical terms, but it is not a substitute for training resources and classes conducted by organizations such as the Associated Locksmiths of America, Lockmasters Security Institute, or any of the other industry-recognized institutions of professional education in this field.

HOW MASTER-KEYING WORKS

I would like to paint for you a picture of a hypothetical office. There are a number of fictional people working there every day, each with their own rights and privileges. We will examine them through a look at their keys and their locks. Hopefully the associated diagrams will help you to follow along. It is my goal that these images will make it at least partially clear to you how master-keying is implemented in basic, pin tumbler locks.

In this office we will begin by examining the keys of four individuals: Alice, Andy, Bob, and Charlie. The first three are general office workers. Alice and Andy have offices right near each other on the same floor. Bob works with somewhat more sensitive information than Alice and Andy, and his office is in another part of the building. Charlie does not have to put on a suit and tie when he goes to work in the morning, as he is part of the maintenance staff. Charlie's duties routinely take him through the area where Alice and Andy work, and his key is able to open all the doors on their floor… but Charlie cannot access Bob's office. In a managerial role is Don, whose space is kept rather private. Only Don and his personal assistant, Dawn, have keys to his corner office. Dawn's key will *only* open Don's office door… but Don's key opens *all* doors. Figure 3.1 shows the keys used by some of these employees. How is this possible?

Situations such as this are achieved by means of master-keying. Simply put, additional pins are installed in some or all of the pin-stacks inside the locks in a master-keyed system, creating more shear lines and thus more combinations of bitting cuts on keys which can potentially operate the locks. Figure 3.2 shows some of the locks in this hypothetical master-keyed system.

Master-keying is a very complicated subject, and I could never hope to cover all of the ways that it can be implemented and achieved. Still, I hope that the following series of diagrams will illustrate why certain users' keys will open only a single door and yet other keys can potentially open multiple doors in this hypothetical office. Figures 3.3 through 3.6 show what will happen if the employees attempt to use their key in multiple doors.

NOTE

Because they are often much smaller in height than key pins or driver pins, you will sometimes hear master pins referred to as "master wafers" in locksmithing circles. While this is a commonly-accepted term (and I can surely see why people choose to use this word), I tend to shy away from such nomenclature. As many of you may know from my first book, *Practical Lock Picking,* there is an entire category of locks known as *wafer locks* which operate on different principles than pin tumbler locks. Wafer mechanisms have little to do with pin tumbler mechanisms, and in an effort to prevent people from ever confusing the two topics, you will always see me refer to "master pins" when I discuss systems like the one being examined in this chapter.

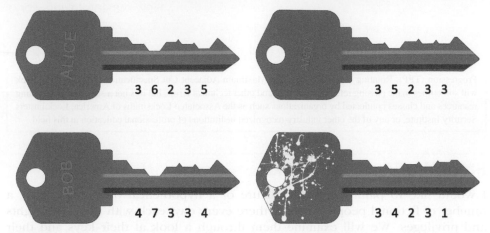

FIGURE 3.1

Here we see the keys belonging to Alice, Andy, Bob, and Charlie. The first three keys are issued to the employees by the Plant Operations staff and have been stamped with the names of their respective users. Charlie's key does not bear his name, but it's often easy to spot a maintenance worker's possessions, given the multitude of stains and splatters to which they are exposed every day. For purposes of clarity (and to help you potentially decode the master-keyed system as we proceed) the bitting codes for each key are printed just below each of them. Bitting codes are specified from the shoulder out toward the tip when read aloud.

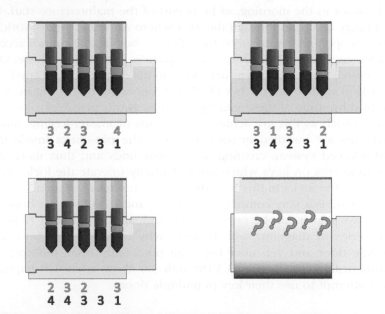

FIGURE 3.2

Here we see some of the locks in this master-keyed system. Each lock makes use of an assortment of key pins (shown in red), driver pins (shown in blue), and a new style of pin which we have yet to examine before now… master pins (shown in teal). Alice's lock and Andy's lock may appear to be somewhat similar in their pinning combinations. This is correct, and we will examine why shortly. The configuration of Don's lock is not revealed at this time, but we will see how it can become possible for any of these employees to gain access to Don's office… even without knowing the exact pinning of his lock.

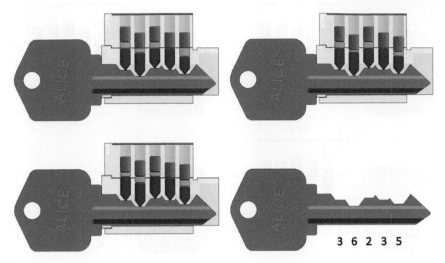

FIGURE 3.3

Here we see Alice trying her key in various office doors. Naturally, this key will operate her lock... in each position, the pin stacks are raised precisely to a shear line. (Note how sometimes this is a shear line atop a key pin and sometimes it is a shear line atop a master pin. This is entirely normal.) Alice's key will not open Andy's lock... in positions #2 and #5 the pin stacks are too "low" and the driver pins are binding. Alice's key will not open Bob's lock... in all but position #4 the pin stacks are out of position, with some raised too high and some remaining too low. In the lower-right we see Alice's key by itself. In a master-keyed system, hers would be known as a *change key* because it grants the least access and can open only a single user's locks.

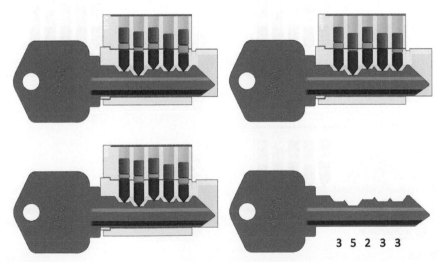

FIGURE 3.4

Here Andy is trying his key in various office doors. Andy's key will not open Alice's lock... it comes close, but in positions #2 and #5 the pin stacks are binding on the teal master pins. Naturally, Andy's key will operate his lock, as can be seen in the upper-right of this diagram. Andy's key will not open Bob's lock... similar to Alice's key before, Andy's key brings virtually none of the pin stacks to heights which will put a shear line at the edge of the plug. In the lower-right we see Andy's key by itself. Much like Alice's, this key is known as a *change key* because it does not grant the user any rights of access beyond their specific office door.

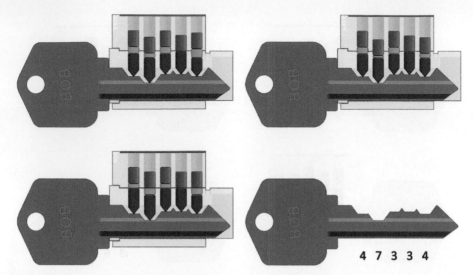

FIGURE 3.5

Here we see Bob trying his key in various office doors. Bob's key will fail to open both Alice's and Andy's locks... in each case, the only pin stack aligned to the proper height by Bob's key is in position #4. Bob's key will, of course, operate his own office door, as can be seen in the lower-left of this diagram. In the lower-right we see Bob's key by itself. As with his co-workers' keys, Bob's is a *change key* because it will operate his door and no others.

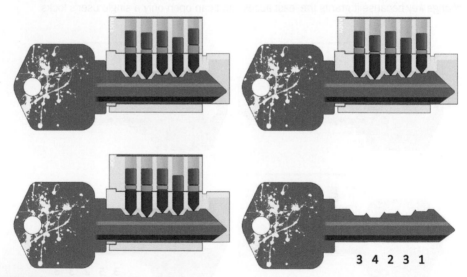

FIGURE 3.6

Here we see Charlie the maintenance man trying his key in various office doors. Because he is authorized to work on their floor, Charlie's key will open both Alice's and Andy's locks. However, Charlie's key will not open Bob's lock. In the lower-right we see Charlie's key by itself. This would be known as an *intermediate master key* because it can operate multiple locks in this system, but not all of them. It is entirely conceivable that a dozen offices could exist on Alice and Andy's floor... each of which could be opened by their own unique change key as well as by Charlie's maintenance key.

In all of the locks in the preceeding images, there exists a *master combination* of pin heights, shared across the entire system. If a key is cut with this master bitting code, it would successfully open *all* of these locks. If you recall, we discussed earlier how Don (the fellow from upper management) has such a key.

ATTACKING MASTER-KEYED SYSTEMS

Imagine that one day Alice becomes disgruntled with her situation at this company. Perhaps she feels that she is underpaid for the amount of work she is doing. Perhaps she has been passed over for promotion too many times. Or perhaps she was involved with Don until their relationship turned sour, leaving her jaded and hurt. Learning of Alice's dissatisfaction with her current employer, a competing company is attempting to lure her away. Making promises of a higher salary, better hours, and longer vacations, this competing firm wins Alice's loyalties. They also dangle before her the possibility of a substantial signing bonus. There's a catch to this last factor, however. The competing firm is prepared to offer Alice this lump sum payment only if she procures internal documents and confidential research from her current employer before leaving her present job.

Ethical considerations aside, how possible would it be for Alice to obtain the proprietary information contained in the secure offices of individuals like Bob? What if she wanted to make one last visit to Don's office, as well, in order to delete emails or otherwise erase any evidence of their previous involvement... could she gain access?

As it turns out, it is rather trivial for Alice to obtain a key which will operate all of the locks in this master-keyed system. Because she is an authorized user of at least *one* of the doors in the system, Alice can use her current key as a basis for escalating her privilege and ultimately creating a top master key. All that is required is a small supply of blank keys and a means of cutting them to various bitting depths.

Blank keys tend to be readily available for most brands of locks, either right off the rack in a hardware store or from locksmithing supply catalogs. Some locks do have what are known as *restricted keyways,* but these are only a minor inconvenience to those seeking a small number of blank keys. Resellers and sites such as eBay often carry "restricted" key blanks, and it is also trivial to fabricate them if one can make use of a device such as the Easy Entrie machine discussed in Chapter 1 and shown in Figure 1.15.

In order to cut keys to the various bitting depths required during this process, an attacker can use locksmithing equipment such as a code-cutting key machine (like the one seen earlier in Figure 1.47) or a manual device known as a *key punch press.* Alternatively, it is also possible for an attacker to simply file keys to various bitting depths with a hand file (of the type used during impressioning) while checking their progress with either a caliper or a key decoder card (like the one seen earlier in Figure 1.67).

Regardless of the equipment used, escalating one's level of privilege and access within a master-keyed system is an attack which can often be executed in less than one hour, using only a handful of keys. Also interesting from a security and monitoring standpoint, is that in our hypothetical office Alice is interested in opening Bob's and Don's doors, but she will perform the bulk of the attack without going anywhere near them. Almost all of her work will be done simply by accessing *her own* door… something that it is perfectly reasonable for her to do many times per day. If a little care is taken, it is doubtful that Alice will look the least bit suspicious as she is preparing to raid an entire company of its intellectual property.

Figure 3.7 shows all that is needed for Alice to begin her attack of the master-keying system in her company's building. She has a key which can successfully open a lock within this system. For purposes of acting covertly, it helps that this is a key she is authorized to possess already. Had she simply obtained another key from elsewhere in the office (one left in the door of a storage closet or a key secretly taken from the desk drawer of another employee, for example) the attack would work in exactly the same manner, but Alice would have to make various trips back to *this other door* during the moments when she needs to test the functionality of a key that has been created at each stage of the process.

Because it is known that Alice's lock can be operated by a key with a code of 3-6-2-3-5 this tells us that all pin stacks are raised to their shear line when a key with this bitting is inserted. If this were a plain lock without any mastering, its internal configuration would appear as shown in Figure 3.8. However, Alice knows that there is master-keying in her lock… she simply does not yet know how it has been implemented.

> **NOTE**
>
> Because virtually all of this attack takes place at Alice's office door as she uses her own key (or modified copies of it) many of the following diagrams will omit the labels above, designating whose locks and keys were whose. All of the diagrams in Figures 3.9 through 3.46 will represent attempted use of keys in Alice's door alone, even though the images are not labeled as such.

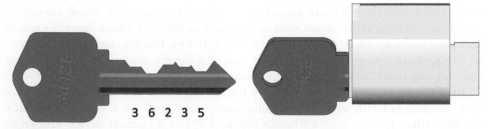

3 6 2 3 5

FIGURE 3.7

Alice has a key which works in at least one lock of the master-keyed system. This is typically all that is ever required to begin a privilege escalation attack.

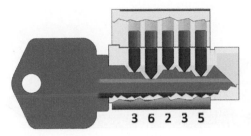
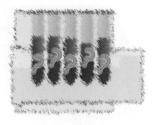

3 6 2 3 5

FIGURE 3.8

If this were a basic, standalone pin tumbler lock with no mastering, it would appear like the lock on the left of this diagram. However, Alice knows there must be master pins present at various positions in her lock… she just does not know where they are. The attack which we will witness in the coming pages will lift away this fog of uncertainty.

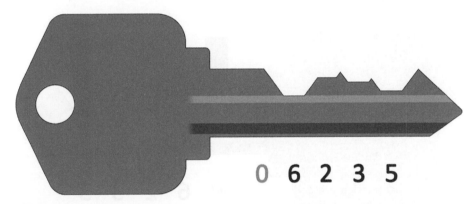

0   6   2   3   5

FIGURE 3.9

This is the first key Alice will use in her exploration of the master-keyed system. It is a close parallel to the key her employer issued to her. It has the same bitting cuts as her change key in positions #2, #3, #4, and #5. Only in position #1 does it differ. Where her original key was cut to a depth of 3 in this position, the current test key has not been cut at all. Thus, this first test key is prepared with a bitting code of 0-6-2-3-5.

As Alice proceeds through her attack, she will use a series of test keys. These keys will be specially-prepared with specific bitting cuts in order to explore each pin stack in search of additional shear lines between pins. The first key that Alice will use is seen in Figure 3.9. It contains the same bitting as the original key her employer issued to her, except in position #1 where the key has not been cut at all.

The idea is for Alice to sweep the entire range of possible bitting depths in the #1 position on her key (see Figure 3.10). By inserting the key, attempting to operate the lock, removing the key, filing it down, and trying again

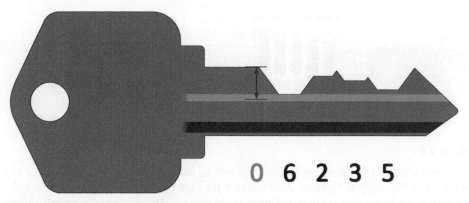

FIGURE 3.10

This is the range through which Alice will search in order to see at which cut depth (or, more likely, cut depths) the key will open the lock.

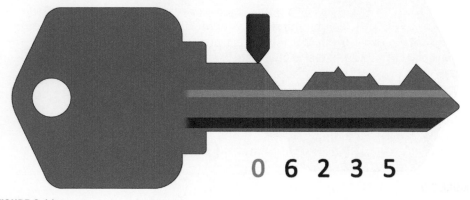

FIGURE 3.11

Currently, this key is in violation of the MACS for this particular brand of lock. (We can tell from the shape of the bow of the key that this is a Kwikset lock, or a clone of that same style. These locks have a MACS value of 4. Thus, a 0-depth cut positioned immediately next to a 6-depth cut is disallowed.)

repeatedly, Alice can determine if there are any other shear lines in this first pin stack inside her lock.

Technically, in its current form this key is in violation of the Maximum Adjacent Cut Specification (MACS) for this particular brand of lock. This book will not delve deeply into matters surrounding MACS restrictions, but Figure 3.11 should convey to you some idea why it is not always possible to have a particularly deep cut situated directly next to a very shallow one. If you wish to be more aware of MACS limitations when you attempt key-based attacks against pin tumbler locks, consult a locksmithing reference book or charts online. One such chart can be found at http://www.locksafesystems.com/depth_and_space.htm

Alice might attempt to use this key in her lock in its current form, but it would almost never function. Indeed, the likelihood of any lock cylinder being pinned to a 0-depth value in *any* position is very rare. For purposes of thoroughness, Alice could indeed give that key a try; it is unlikely to ever do any harm. The real work of searching through this first pin position, however, will begin when this first test key is modified by starting to file down (the upcoming figures illustrate how the attack would look if conducted with a hand file) in position #1 (see Figure 3.12). Technically this key is still not in compliance with MACS rules (see Figure 3.13), but since she is attempting to search across a combination of master bitting depths and user-level bitting depths it would be a good idea for Alice to attempt to use this key in her door right now.

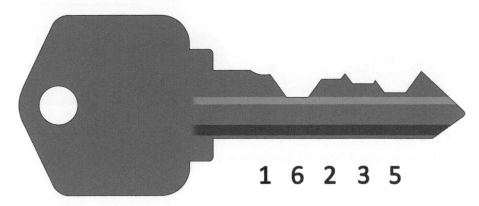

FIGURE 3.12

The real process of a master-key searching attack will begin with the filing down of position #1 to a 1-cut depth.

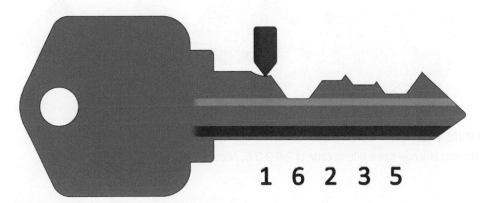

FIGURE 3.13

This key is still in violation of MACS rules, but Alice will try it in her door anyway.

The key which has been cut and filed to a bitting code of 1-6-2-3-5 is inserted into Alice's door. She attempts to turn it, and finds that it does not work (see Figure 3.14).

Alice removes the key and files it down some more in the #1 position. Again, these images show how the attack would look if the key were being manually filed, but this attack could be performed just as easily (indeed, some people would say that it might go much more smoothly) if the key were being modified each time using a code-cutting machine or a punch press. With the key now cut to a depth value of 2 in the #1 position, Alice is ready to try again (see Figures 3.15 and 3.16).

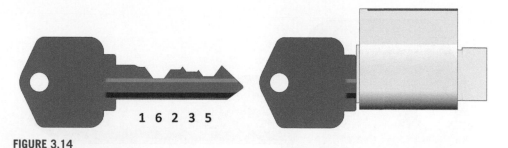

1 6 2 3 5

FIGURE 3.14

A key with a bitting code of 1-6-2-3-5 does not work in Alice's door.

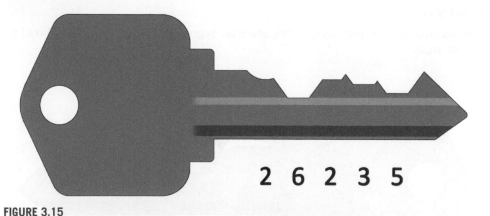

2 6 2 3 5

FIGURE 3.15

The test key now has a bitting code of 2-6-2-3-5. Alice is ready to try it in her door again.

Alice removes the key and files it down further in the #1 position. With the key now cut to a depth value of 3 in the #1 position, Alice is ready to try again. She expects the key to function when she tries it this time. Do you know why? See Figure 3.17 to learn whether or not Alice is correct.

Although it was expected that the lock would open when this 3-6-2-3-5 key was inserted, Alice has now learned something significant. She is now aware that a key pin is inserted in this #1 position and that it is a height of 3. Since Alice has searched slowly through the depths up to this point, she knows that this first pin is solid, with no intermediate shear lines. If there *are* additional

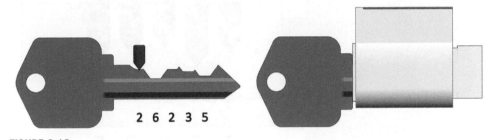

2 6 2 3 5

FIGURE 3.16

A key with bitting code 2-6-2-3-5 does not violate MACS. It fails to work in Alice's door, however.

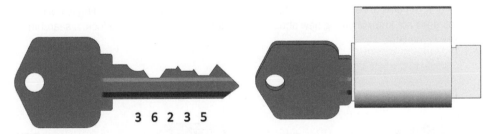

3 6 2 3 5

FIGURE 3.17

Alice's assumptions were correct, and her test key now successfully operates the lock in its current shape. This should come as little surprise... the key now has the same bitting code, 3-6-2-3-5, as her originally-issued key. Alice could have just as easily skipped past this depth while searching pin stack #1. Perhaps she simply wanted to verify that she was doing a good job while filing the key and is now relieved to see that indeed she is creating the cuts exactly as required to carry out this searching process.

shear lines (caused by an additional mastering pin) in this first position, they must be higher up in the pin stack (see Figure 3.18)

Alice removes her key, files position #1 down to the next depth (a bitting value of 4), and again tries the key in the lock. It fails to open (see Figure 3.19).

Although it was expected that the lock would open when this 3-6-2-3-5 key was inserted, Alice has now learned something significant. She is now aware that there will be something "above" her first pin and that it is a height of 3 above the key cut at depth #1 she was filing up to this point, she knows that this first pin stack has one or more false shear lines. If there are additional

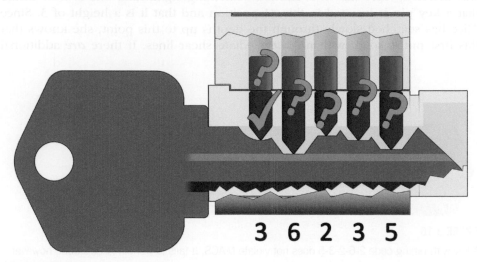

3 6 2 3 5

FIGURE 3.18

Alice has established that the first pin in the "bottom" of the front stack is a key pin with a size value of 3. It remains to be seen what is "above" that pin, and thus more searching is needed. Alice still does not know anything new about the pin stacks deeper within the lock... searching those will come later.

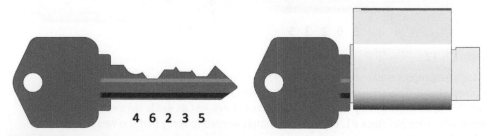

4 6 2 3 5

FIGURE 3.19

The first bitting position on the key is filed down a bit further, resulting in an overall bitting code of 4-6-2-3-5. With this bitting, the key does not operate the lock.

She removes the key, files down a little more, and tries the key again. It still fails to open (see Figure 3.20).

Undaunted, Alice continues the process. She files position #1 down a little further on her key, resulting in an overall bitting code of 6-6-2-3-5. She tries the key in her office door lock. It opens! (See Figure 3.21.) Alice has now discovered a shear line in this first pin stack which was previously unknown (see Figure 3.22).

Since she already knows the bitting of her change key, and because the lock is operating with the #1 pin stack in an entirely different position than the one she is used to using, Alice can rather safely conclude that she has found a *master cut depth* in this first pin stack. If she is taking notes, she might jot down a bitting code of 6-?-?-?-? as if to indicate that while the rest of the lock still remains a mystery, a depth value of 6 in the #1 position is likely the master-keyed value.

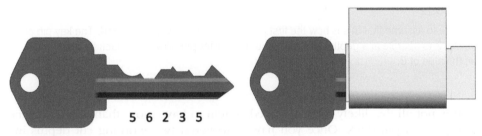

5 6 2 3 5

FIGURE 3.20

The first bitting position on the key is filed down further, resulting in a key with a bitting code of 5-6-2-3-5. The key does not operate the lock.

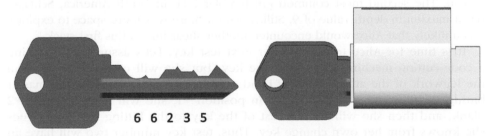

6 6 2 3 5

FIGURE 3.21

When filed down to a bitting of 6-6-2-3-5, the key opens Alice's door lock. She has now likely discovered a master cut depth for this first position.

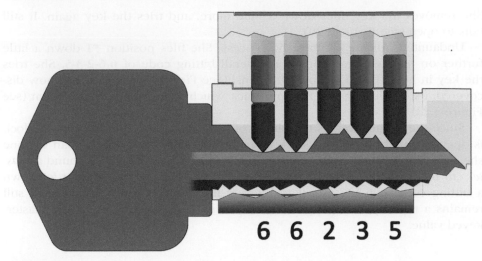

FIGURE 3.22

It is safe to assume that this is how the first pin stack in the lock is configured. The key pin allows the stack to operate at a depth value of 3, and the master pin allows the stack to operate at a depth value of 6.

It is not all that likely for a mastered system to have more than two shear lines in any given pin stack. Once you have discovered two working cut depths in a particular position, you are usually done and can often safely move on. However, if she wishes to be extra-diligent, Alice might opt to cut this key down one final time. Filing the #1 position to a depth of 7, she tries the key in her lock. It fails to open (see Figure 3.23). Alice can stop here, because a bitting value of 7 is the maximum depth for Kwikset-style locks. Many locks can be cut deeper, of course. The second most common pin tumbler lock in North America, Schlage, has a maximum depth value of 9. Still... even if there was more space to explore, it is unlikely that Alice would encounter another shear line in this first stack.

It is time for Alice to prepare her next test key. Let's assume she is using a code-cutting machine to prepare the key (but she will continue to perform the legwork of the attack itself by hand, with a file). Alice will use the master bitting depth which she discovered in position #1, she will leave position #2 blank, and then she will cut the rest of the key to the bitting working values she knows from her own change key. Thus, test key number two will have an initial bitting of 6-0-2-3-5 (see Figure 3.24).

Whether or not Alice tries this key in her lock right now is just a matter of personal choice. As mentioned before, it is highly unlikely that the locks in her company's master-keyed system will make use of a 0-depth cut in any position. She may opt to simply file the key to a depth of 1 in the #2 position right off the bat (see Figure 3.25). She might even have used a code-cutter to create

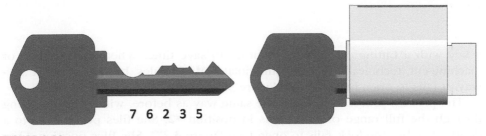

FIGURE 3.23

Just for closure, Alice might try to file down further and see if the lock operates with a bitting depth of 7 in the #1 position. It does not open. Alice is now done in this first position because Kwikset-style locks do not have any depths beyond 7.

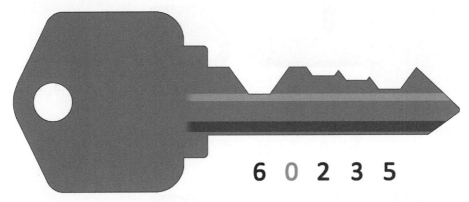

FIGURE 3.24

The second test key to be used in this attack will begin with a bitting code of 6-0-2-3-5. Alice is going to sweep the full range of depths in position #2 this time.

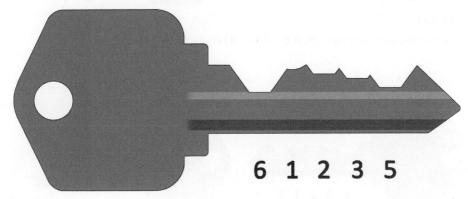

FIGURE 3.25

A bitting value of 6-1-2-3-5 is likely to be the real start of where Alice begins her search of working cut depths in position #2.

a key with a bitting of 6-1-2-3-5 in order to save time. Whether hand-filed or machine-cut, technically this key still violates MACS rules, but Alice tries it anyway. It fails to open her lock (see Figure 3.26).

The process proceeds in much the same way as before, with Alice sweeping through the full range of cut depths in position #2. She files position #2 to a depth of 2, but the lock fails to open (see Figure 3.27). She files position #2 to a depth of 3, but the lock fails to open (see Figure 3.28). She files position #2 to a depth of 4, and discovers that the key suddenly works (see Figure 3.29).

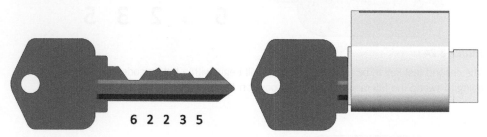

FIGURE 3.26

MACS is still being violated with this key, but Alice tries it anyway. It does not open the lock.

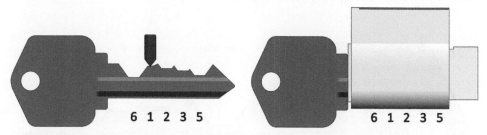

FIGURE 3.27

Alice tries a key with a bitting code of 6-2-2-3-5. It fails to open the lock.

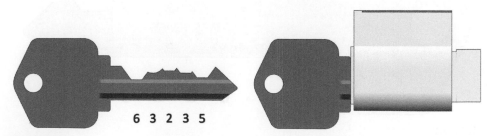

FIGURE 3.28

Alice tries a key with a bitting code of 6-3-2-3-5. It fails to open the lock.

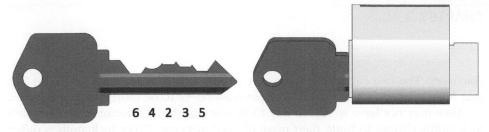

FIGURE 3.29

Alice tries a key with a bitting code of 6-4-2-3-5. The lock opens!

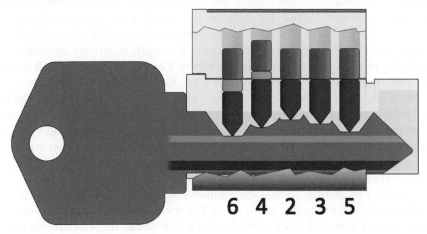

FIGURE 3.30

A cut depth of 4 in position #2 allowed the lock to turn, thus Alice knows that pin stack #2 likely looks like this… with a key pin of size 4 and a master pin of size 2 above it. She knows this because of the cut depth on her original key.

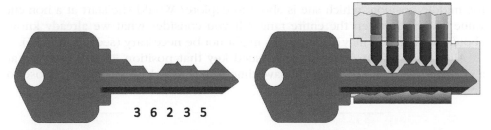

FIGURE 3.31

Alice's original key had a depth value of 6 in position #2. She knows that position #2 must operate at a depth of 4 as well as 6, and has concluded that the pin stack must look like what is seen here. Still nothing is known about the rear three pin stacks, however.

Alice has now successfully discovered yet another new working cut depth in the lock: the lock will function if position #2 is cut to a depth of 4 (see Figure 3.30). She also knows (from her original key) that the lock will function if position #2 is cut to a depth of 6 (see Figure 3.31). This is a very significant discovery. The two cut positions are very close together. They are so close, in fact, that Alice may consider her search of pin position #2 to be more or less complete.

Alice may not have to search any further in position #2 because of how many locksmiths choose to build their master-keyed systems. Every locksmith is differ-ent, of course, but many of them (I might even go so far as to say the majority of them) do not like to use master pins with a size value of 1. Master pins of this size are exceedingly thin (hence the emergence of the term *master wafer...* a term I choose not to use for reasons explained previously) and can cause problems within a lock. They are more susceptible to damage, and they can also "flip" within the pin chamber, becoming caught sideways or falling down through the plug in certain unlikely situations. I'm not saying you will never see them in the field, but master pins of size 1 are less common than others.

Thus, if we were to consider what a working 5-depth or 7-depth in position #2 would entail, we would see that the *only* way these cuts could be valid would be through the use of size 1 master pins (see Figure 3.32). I'm not saying you'll never see size 1 master pins in a system (if you look back at Figure 3.2 you will see that even I could not easily avoid using one of them in Andy's lock), but encountering a *series* of these tiny pins is not very common. If Alice is writing notes to herself about master key bitting codes, she probably would not be wrong to jot down the digits 6-4-?-?-? and simply move on. If for some reason she fails to discover a working master key and has to double-check her work, she can always return to position #2 and search through the rest of these discarded values.

It is time for Alice to prepare a third test key. She believes that she has dis-covered master bitting values in the first two positions, and thus will start her bitting code with 6-4. She is not currently working on the two deepest positions; she will leave them set to her initial change key bitting values of 3-5. But what of the middle position, which she is about to explore? Would she start at a non-cut value of 0 and sweep the entire range? If you consider what we already know about the lock, you may see how this might not be necessary (see Figure 3.33).

Alice knows from her company-issued key that position #3 will function at a cut depth of 2. If she wants to save time in her search, Alice might choose to

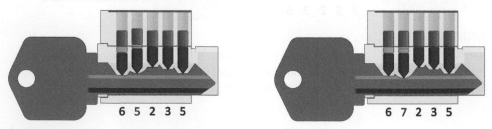

6 5 2 3 5   6 7 2 3 5

FIGURE 3.32

The only way a 5-depth or 7-depth would be valid in position #2 is if that stack includes master pins with a size of 1. Since these are less common, Alice might opt to skip searching any further in this position and simply move on.

skip searching at the depth of 2. If she wants to be *very* efficient, Alice might also cross off the values directly above and below 2 (because for them to be valid, size 1 master pins would have to be involved). We have discussed the fact that a 0-depth cut is almost *never* going to be seen on a real world key. Thus, Alice could conceivably begin her search in position #3 with a depth value of 4, and sweep the range from there down (see Figures 3.34 and 3.35).

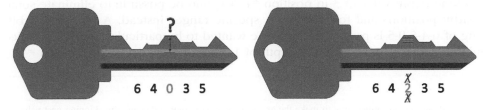

FIGURE 3.33

Would Alice truly have to sweep the full range from 0 to 7 in this third pin position as she searches for a master cut depth? Since she already knows that 2 is a working value, she might choose to skip 1, 2, and 3 entirely.

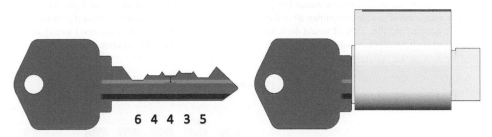

FIGURE 3.34

Alice might simply start with a code-cut key that has a bitting of 6-4-4-3-5 while she searches through position #3. This bitting value fails to operate the lock, however.

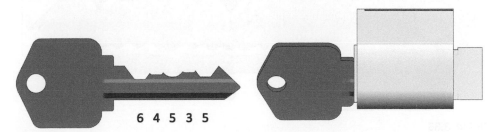

FIGURE 3.35

Alice files position #3 down slightly, to a depth of 5. The key opens the lock!

As we can see in Figure 3.35, when Alice files position #3 down to a depth of 5, the lock opens. Thus, she has built an even more revealing picture of the internals of her door (see Figure 3.36). Alice has now most likely discovered the master cut depths for three of the five pin positions in her lock. She revises her hand-written notes with the figures *6-4-5-?-?* and procures yet another blank to prepare as her next test key.

A fourth testing key now must be prepared. What range would Alice have to explore here? As Figure 3.37 attempts to illustrate, because of the known working depth value of 3 in position #4, it would be possible to eliminate some nearby positions and focus only on specific ranges instead. A key with a bitting of 6-4-5-0-5 is prepared, but if she wanted to be particularly efficient, Alice might choose to only test a cut depth of 1, then of 5 through 7 in position #4.

TIP

All of these hints regarding how to make the exploratory process more efficient—by skipping past values which would necessitate the use of size 1 master pins—are, in my opinion, only sensible advice if you have to return to a code-cutting machine or key punch press every step of the way. If you have to frequently leave the vicinity of the lock which you are exploring (in order to walk outside to your vehicle each time in order to access your key-cutting hardware, or if the lock you are inspecting is not on your own door but is in a location which you have to make an excuse to go visit), it may make sense for you to attempt to save time by skipping past some less-likely depths.

However, if you are executing a master key privilege escalation attack on a door to which you have easy, regular access and if you are performing all of the key cutting right there at the same location (for instance, if you are using a hand file)… then I would think that thoroughness should trump efficiency and I would advise you to test each cut depth anyway. What is it really going to cost you? Five to ten additional minutes?

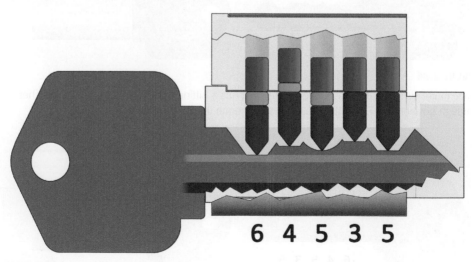

FIGURE 3.36

Alice has likely now discovered the master cut depths for more than half of her lock. And, of course, she is not simply discovering details of her own lock… master cut depths usually apply to all locks across the whole system.

Following her "efficiency" model, Alice tries her key, with position #4 cut to depths 1, 3, 5, 6, and 7. The lock only opens when the key is filed to a depth of 3 and no other shear lines are discovered (see Figures 3.38 through 3.42).

The results of exploring pin position #4 might puzzle and confuse Alice. In a master-keyed system it is normal to expect to encounter more than one shear line in each pin stack. But nothing other than the depth of 3 (which was already known from her original change key) was found to work. Should Alice go back and try again with a fresh key? Should she be more careful and

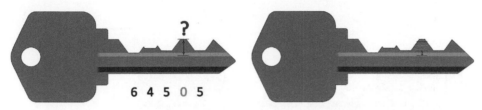

FIGURE 3.37

Because Alice knows one working cut depth in position #4 (she knows from her original key that a depth of 3 is valid in this position) she might opt to *not* inspect depths of 2 or 4, since each would indicate the presence of a size 1 master pin.

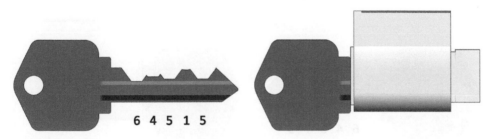

FIGURE 3.38

A key filed to a bitting of 6-4-5-1-5 is tried in the lock. It fails to open.

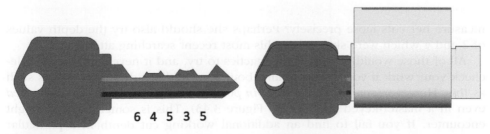

FIGURE 3.39

A key filed to a bitting of 6-4-5-3-5 is tried in the lock. It opens as expected.

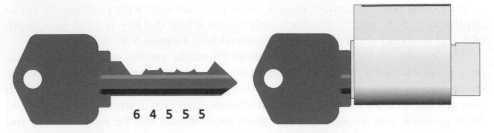

FIGURE 3.40

A key filed to a bitting of 6-4-5-5-5 is tried in the lock. It fails to open.

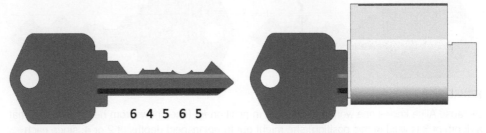

FIGURE 3.41

A key filed to a bitting of 6-4-5-6-5 is tried in the lock. It fails to open.

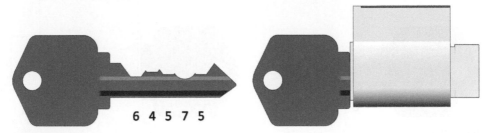

FIGURE 3.42

A key filed to a bitting of 6-4-5-7-5 is tried in the lock. It fails to open.

measure her cuts more precisely? Perhaps she should also try the depth values of 2 and 4 which were skipped on this most recent searching attempt.

All of those would be appropriate tactics to try, and it never hurts to double-check your work if you are uncertain about your findings during a process such as this. However, *sometimes certain pin positions simply are not master-pinned even in a master-keyed system* (see Figure 3.43). This is something you might encounter. If you fail to find an additional working cut depth in a particular position on a key when searching for master bitting codes, sometimes you just

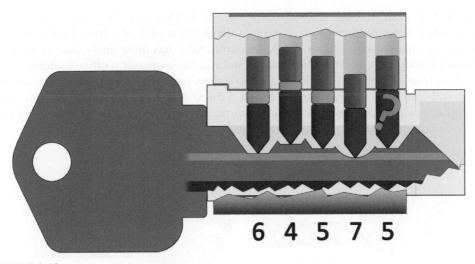

FIGURE 3.43

Even in master-keyed systems, some pin stacks may simply not be mastered. If you fail to find more than one working cut depth in a particular position (especially if you check more than once) you may not be doing anything wrong. Simply record the single known bitting value (from your change key) as possibly being part of the master bitting code and move on.

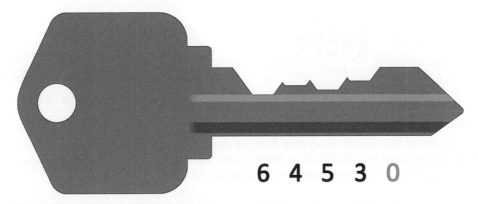

FIGURE 3.44

This is the final test key that Alice is likely to require for her attack.

have to note it down and move on. If Alice is amending her written notes, she would likely record a code of 6-4-5-3-?, indicating that only the final pin position remains to be explored.

Alice's attack is nearing its conclusion. She prepares a final testing key, with a bitting code of 6-4-5-3-0 (see Figure 3.44). The very tip of the key, position #5, is all that remains to be explored. Alice tries the key as it is right now, not expecting the lock to turn. Indeed, it would have been a shock to see the 0-cut depth function. Alice files the #5 position down to a depth value of 1. She tries the key in the lock… it opens! (See Figure 3.45.) At this time, Alice has most likely discovered the master bitting code for the whole lock system in her company's office building.

It is true that plenty of searching nevertheless could be done in the #5 position. But still… if I were executing this attack, I'd just immediately start trying this key in other doors. (Or perhaps I would generate a fresh copy of the 6-4-5-3-1 key on a code-cutting machine, as seen in Figure 3.46, and try *that* in all of the doors.)

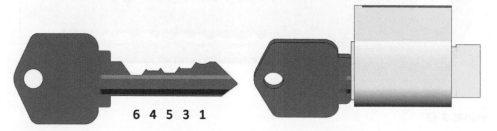

FIGURE 3.45

What luck! When she filed position #5 down to a depth of 1 the key worked! It is very possible that Alice has now discovered the master key bitting for the whole lock system.

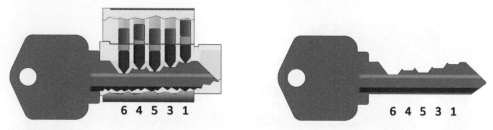

FIGURE 3.46

The left side of this diagram shows what Alice has most likely achieved within her door lock. If she wishes to test her bitting code on the rest of the building, it might make sense to prepare a fresh key using a code cutting machine, as shown on the right.

TIP

If Alice was performing the entire attack without *any* use of a code-cutting machine or a key punch press, then her resultant master key might look more like what can be seen in Figure 3.47. While this will indeed work, the round-bottomed cuts generated by the types of files shown in Chapter 1 are not always the most desirable when you are performing a master-key privilege escalation attack. If you have the ability to, try to "flatten" out the bottom of your cuts so that the pins settle into their ideal positions.

Also, whenever you are filing by hand, always remain aware of the problem of "canyoning" which was also described in Chapter 1 when we discussed impressioning (see Figure 3.48). Getting your key stuck in a lock is absolutely not something you want to have happen, particularly if you are trying to be covert while you carry out this type of attack!

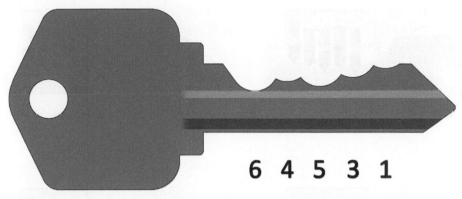

FIGURE 3.47

Hand-filed keys are likely to have very rounded cuts in each position. It may be more helpful if you attempt to "flatten" your cuts somehow, although this is not always possible with most files you are likely to have in your tool kit.

FIGURE 3.48

Always be aware of the problem of "canyoning" your cuts. If you are not careful, it is possible to get a key stuck inside of a lock with little or no way to remove it while the lock is mounted in a door.

If Alice were to take her newly-discovered master key and try it in other doors around the office, she is likely to be very successful in gaining access everywhere. Not only will it open her own door (which we have already seen) but it will also open Andy's door down the hall. If Alice were to proceed to Bob's office, in the secure wing of the building where not even Charlie has access, she will find that her key works there, too. Even Don's office door is

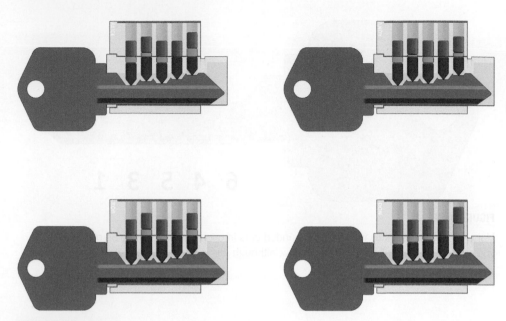

FIGURE 3.49

The top master key which Alice has successfully decoded will allow her to access all offices in the building, including Don's executive corner office.

SPECIAL READER CHALLENGE: Assuming Dawn (Don's personal assistant) has a change key that opens *only* his door and none other, can anyone here take careful measurements of the pins in these images (which are all to scale) and tell me what the bitting code of Dawn's key would be? Email me at deviant@deviating.net if you think you know the answer. The first person to answer correctly wins a prize.

found to offer no resistance. Figure 3.49 illustrates all of these doors which are now compromised, even though it is the very first time that Alice is likely approaching any of them.

OTHER METHODS OF MASTER KEY COMPROMISE

As you can see, the risks are very real for a rogue employee or even an intruder compromising the top master key of a lock system if they have access to a single working key and the lock that it operates. However, a privilege escalation attack is most surely not the only means by which a master-keyed system can be compromised.

In a master-keyed environment, virtually *all* of the locks will have the master cut depths present within their cylinders. This means that if an attacker can acquire and disassemble any lock in the system, they can potentially observe, photograph, or measure the pins within in order to determine the master key bitting. Figures 3.50 and 3.51 are photographs taken during penetration testing

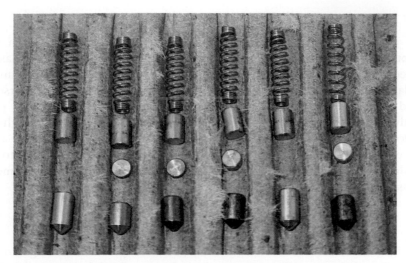

FIGURE 3.50

These pin stacks are from a master-keyed lock which was disassembled and examined during a penetration test in July 2008.

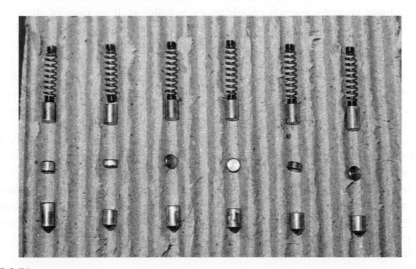

FIGURE 3.51

These pin stacks are from a master-keyed lock which was disassembled and examined during a penetration test in March 2010.

jobs, showing the inner workings of locks which were hastily disassembled and laid out on makeshift pin trays (made from torn pieces of corrugated cardboard).

If you are thinking about attempting to take a lock from a target facility in order to inspect its internal pin configuration and you wish to be covert about it, I would offer the following advice.

Target a lock no one will miss

If you encounter a door in a disused area, it might be the one from which you opt to remove the lock. Even better, if you can find a door that has been removed or a lock that is otherwise not in use at all, this could be an ideal candidate for you to take and inspect at your leisure. Beware, of course, that disused hardware may not be current and could possibly not even be part of the active master-keyed system. Also, just because a lock is not in a high-traffic area does not mean no one uses it. Store rooms, attics, and supply closets all have their purpose... and the types of people who need to get into these spaces might even be *more* likely than the general public to notice something is amiss.

Target a lock that is rarely used

This might be a wiser course of action, provided you can manage to make it work. Try to temporarily acquire a lock from a door that is rarely, if ever, secured. The best example I can give of this phenomenon is that of restroom doors. Many lavatories in schools, offices, and other large institutions have locks on them. How often do you see them actually secured? While some facilities may have security guards checking each toilet stall as part of their nightly patrol, it is *very* rare for them to conclude their stop in the washroom by locking the deadbolt on their way out. During daytime hours, locked bathrooms are even less likely (save for perhaps times when they are undergoing cleaning or maintenance... but even then, a yellow A-frame plastic sign placed in front of the door is far more common than use of the lock itself). If you can manage to remove a bathroom lock it is likely that no one would ever notice, provided that you temporarily replace it with a suitable stand-in.

Quickly swapping out the door lock on a public restroom is likely to be something that no one will detect, unless you are spotted during the actual moment you are unscrewing and removing the hardware itself. Of course, quick-release door handles are becoming increasingly popular in institutional environments, precisely because of how easily they can be serviced. Learn how these mechanisms function, keep a spare lock core in your pocket, and you could potentially be walking away with an entire company's master key codes in under 30 seconds.

DEFENDING AGAINST THIS ATTACK

Unfortunately, the methods of defending against this sort of attack are very limited, at least with regard to conventional pin-tumbler lock hardware. By their very nature, lock systems controlled by a single top master key at the very highest point on their planning charts offer a single point of compromise to an attacker. This makes for a very tempting target.

Some security experts advise that it may be best to split your facility into entirely distinct mastering systems, so that intermediate master and top master keys which service one portion of a campus or building have no rights of access in other areas. I regularly encourage companies to secure their *most* sensitive resources with locks that are entirely separate from the master-keyed system. The handful of people who need access to a server room or records room or financial office can be burdened with carrying a single additional key... I feel that this is a minor inconvenience which is far outweighed by the benefits of additional security.

Some people take may comfort in the fact that their lock systems rely on "restricted" keyways for which the supply of blank keys is not as abundant. While this does indeed make the execution of a privilege escalation attack nontrivial, I do not believe that unique keyways alone can prevent it entirely.

In *Rights Amplification in Master-Keyed Mechanical Locks,* Matt Blaze listed different kinds of mastering systems (such as master rings, bicentric cylinders, and other more exotic hardware) which are not susceptible to these styles of attack. While not mentioned in Blaze's paper, I have a particular fondness for disc-detainer lock systems, such as the products offered by the Abloy company of Finland, now a part of the renowned ASSA/Abloy Group.

Disc-based locks (like the utterly wonderful Abloy Protec) can be configured in a mastered fashion, and such a system does *not* allow for privilege escalation attacks. In fact, because of the way mastering works with disc-based padlocks, even the direct compromise and disassembly of a lower-level lock in the system will not reveal the details necessary to compromise higher-permission keys which would grant access to more secure areas. Very few dealers carry these kinds of locks, and even among those who do, not everyone is well-versed in custom-keying a whole system with mastered permissions. Two vendors who *can* provide Abloy Protec locks in a wide variety of mastered combinations are Securty Snobs in the United States (http://securitysnobs.com, @SecuritySnobs on Twitter) and Han Fey Lock Technologies in the Netherlands (http://hanfey-locktechnologies.com).

Electro-mechanical locks which incorporate circuitry and microchips also often can provide all manner of advanced access controls including time-restricted access, mastering, and audit logging. Of course, there is the whole separate issue of how secure the electronic elements are within the lock, but that is outside of the scope of this book. If you wish to know more about electro-mechanical locks, you could always search for a presentation given by Babak Javadi and I at the DeepSec conference in Austria in 2010. Video from that presentation is available online from a number of sites.

MAISON-KEYING

One final point that I feel I should convey in this chapter concerns locks which incorporate the exact opposite of master-keying. Locks with what is known as *maison-keying* are sometimes found in condominiums, apartments, or dormitories.

Unlike master-keying, where a single key can open many locks, maison keying is a system in which a single *lock* can be opened by many *keys*. This is achieved either by using a *very* limited number of pin stacks in a maison-keyed lock (I have seen a front gate of an apartment complex, for example, which featured only two pin stacks!) or by incorporating so many master pins per stack that there are virtually dozens of valid bitting combinations.

As you can imagine, maison-keying is not very secure. It might be acceptable for something like a laundry room or exercise room, or for a pool-access gate in a shared space like a dormitory or housing complex, but I would not advise maison-keying for the front of any office building or other perimeter-access control door.

SUMMARY

This chapter explored the means by which master-keying is most commonly achieved in pin tumbler lock systems. As the examples and diagrams in this chapter illustrated, it is actually quite difficult to implement a master-keyed system without sacrificing some degree of security in the process. Greater likelihood of lockpicking attempts being successful, as well as overall susceptibility to key-escalation attacks or decoding of the pins if a lock is disassembled, are the risks with which you must contend if you desire the convenience of master keys.

Privilege escalation attacks can usually be carried out by anyone who has been given authorized access (by means of a change key) to even just one of the locks in a master-keyed system. By means of trial-and-error, along with considerable estimated guessing and use of insider knowledge, an attacker can often discover the master-keying depth values with less than one or two hours of overall effort, requiring only a small supply of blank keys and a means with which to cut them. Also, direct compromise of any lock in the system can lead to disclosure of the master-keying depth values if said lock is disassembled and inspected.

It is possible to reduce or outright eliminate the threat of attack against a master-keyed system, but such solutions typically either involve a move away from the conventional pin-tumbler style of lock or must sacrifice some degree of flexibility and convenience within the master-keyed system itself (by use of separate mastering domains or the complete exclusion of certain high-value doors from the mastering system).

Bump Keys

4

CHAPTER OUTLINE

INTRODUCTION

Due to the way in which pin tumbler locks function and how their internal components interact, a number of tools exist which can cause a large percentage of these locks to open almost immediately if the right forces are applied with a little care and some precise timing. The techniques of snapping and bumping have been known to locksmiths for years; in the past decade they have also been seeing increased exposure in the press, news media, and as topics of discussion at security conferences.

Many people are amazed when they learn just how straightforward and uncomplicated these attacks are. Because they rely on very simple laws of physics to quickly spring locks open, tactics like snapping and bumping can be a boon to penetration testers, police, and other operatives who seek to quickly enter a facility without the need for a great deal of finesse.

SNAPPING ATTACKS

Occasionally featured on TV programs about crime or espionage (and often listed in the back pages of spy publications and soldier-of-fortune catalogs) are tools known as *pick guns*, also known as *snapper guns* or *snapping guns*. These tools feature a long trigger handle which, when pulled, will retract and

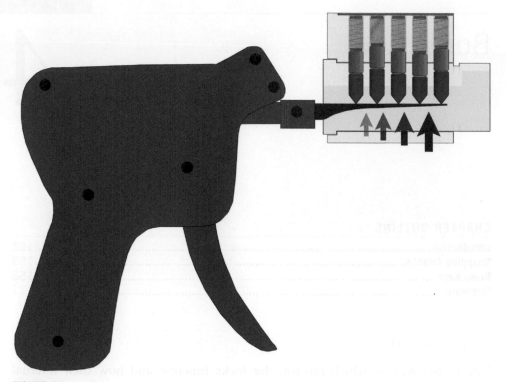

FIGURE 4.1

A pick gun or snap gun is designed to be held such that the long needle-like arm flies toward the pin stacks, contacting the key pins.

then quickly release a needle-like arm. This arm is designed to be inserted into the keyway of a pin tumbler lock and held such that it will smack into the exposed surfaces of the key pins when the "snap" takes place, as shown in Figure 4.1.

In an ideal world, the resultant strike against the pin stacks will take place across all key pins in the same instant and with relatively the same force, as depicted in Figure 4.2. Newtonian laws of motion tell us that, like balls on a billiard table (such as the ones seen in Figure 4.3), energy should transfer through the key pins (see Figure 4.4) and result in movement of the driver pins. If you're lucky, the driver pins will fly "upward" (see Figure 4.5) allowing you to turn the plug if you time everything perfectly.

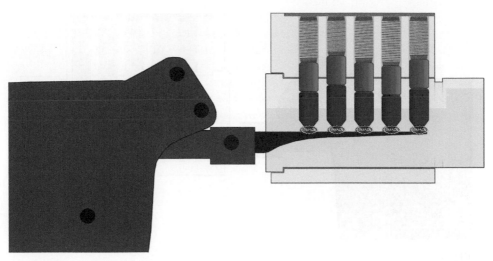

FIGURE 4.2

When using a pick gun, one attempts to make the needle arm contact all of the tips of the key pins simultaneously. This is often very difficult. Not only must the pick gun be held perfectly level, but there has to be enough room within the keyway for the arm to travel. This is less and less common on modern, well-engineered keyways.

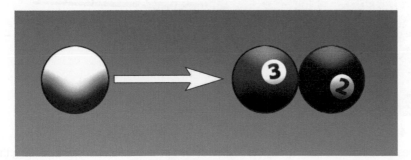

FIGURE 4.3

Lock snapping (and bumping, for that matter) relies on basic principles of Newtonian physics, which can be illustrated via the transfer of energy between balls on a billiard table.

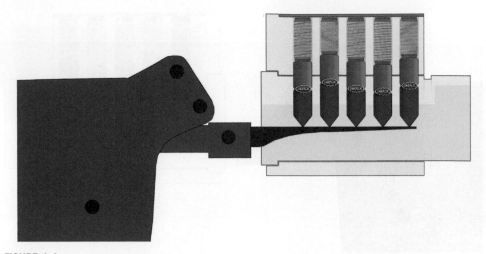

FIGURE 4.4

Ideally, energy that is delivered to the key pins will transfer through to the driver pins.

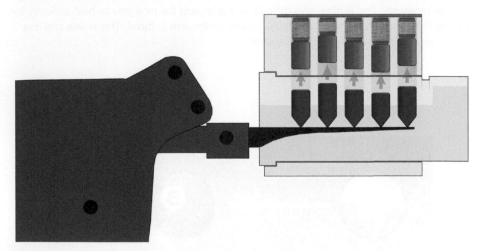

FIGURE 4.5

If all goes well, the driver pins will fly out of their default positions for an instant, allowing the lock's plug to turn.

BUMP KEYS

As mentioned in the description of Figure 4.2 those attempting to use pick guns will often experience difficulty if the needle arm doesn't contact all of the key pins at exactly the same moment and deliver adequate force. It is quite possible, however, to replicate this same physical force using a device that is much smaller, more clandestine, and (in my opinion) easier to operate. I am speaking about a bump key.

What makes a key a bump key?

A bump key, in its most basic form, is nothing more than a key that is designed for the keyway profile of a specific lock and which has had each of its bitting positions (see Figure 4.6) cut down to a particularly deep level (see Figure 4.7). Occasionally, this type of cutting can result in a particularly large rise of metal near the tip of the key blade (also visible in Figure 4.7). If this ever happens, it is often advisable to make an additional bitting cut (at an equally deep level) in one further position (as shown in Figure 4.8). If you have access to a lock-smith's code-cutting machine, this is achieved on most brands of keys by programming the cuts to be a depth of "9" in every position. (It is for this reason that a bump key is sometimes called a "999" key.)

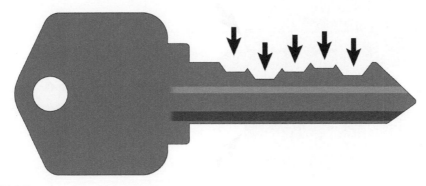

FIGURE 4.6

The bitting positions on a normal key are all evenly-spaced along the blade.

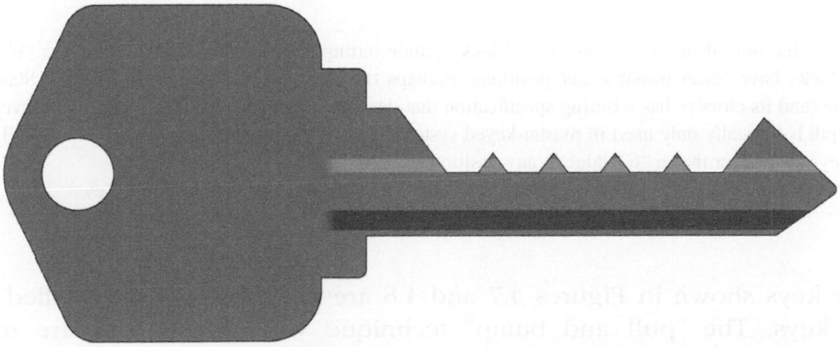

FIGURE 4.7

On a bump key those same bitting positions (as seen in Figure 4.6) are used, but the cuts are made to a much deeper level. Typically, each position is cut to its factory-deepest setting.

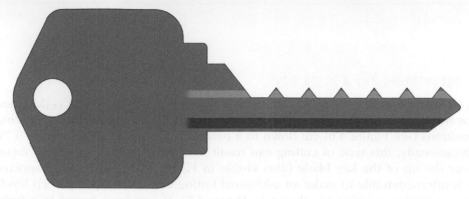

FIGURE 4.8

To eliminate the large "hump" of metal which is sometime seen on the tip of a bump key (one is visible in Figure 4.7) an additional bitting position can be cut into the key blade out near the tip.

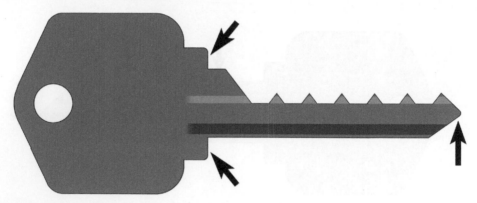

FIGURE 4.9

Additional metal is removed at these points on a "pull" bump key to turn it into a "push" bump key.

NOTE

Be aware that not all makes and models of lock include bitting specifications all the way to a "9" depth. Some locks have fewer possible cut positions. Perhaps the most typical lock in the United States, the Kwikset (and its clones), has a bitting specification that does not enumerate past a "7" cut... and even then, this depth is typically only used in master-keyed systems. Nearly all off-the-shelf Kwikset locks will never have keys cut deeper than a "6" value in any position.

Thus, technically, a KW1 or KW10 bump key would be a "666" or possibly a "777" key.

The keys shown in Figures 4.7 and 4.8 are of a type typically called "pull" bump keys. The "pull and bump" technique with which they are used is depicted in Figures 4.11 through 4.13. Some people, however, choose to modify their bump keys even further. By removing additional metal around the shoulder and tip of the key (see Figure 4.9) it is possible to make a "push"

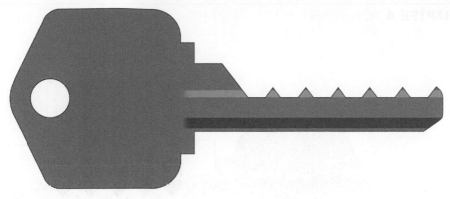

FIGURE 4.10

A "push" style bump key. Also known as a "negative shoulder" or "minimal movement" bump key.

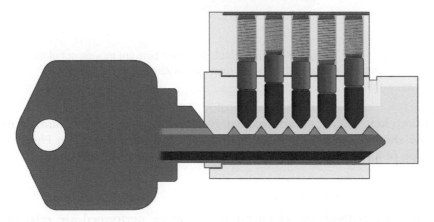

FIGURE 4.11

A bump key in position for a "pull and bump" attempt. It has been pulled out by "one click" and is ready to be struck.

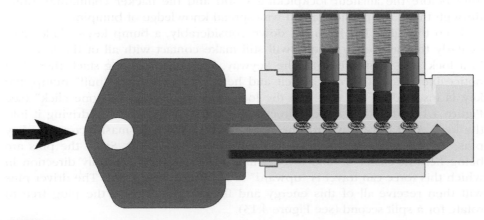

FIGURE 4.12

As the strike comes, the bump key moves into the lock, smashing across the key pins as it does so.

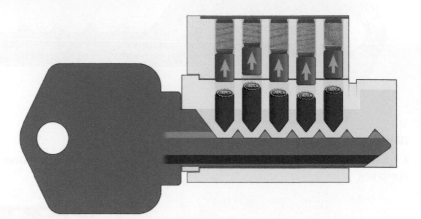

FIGURE 4.13

This looks to be a successful bump attempt; the driver pins are moving out of their default positions, hopefully allowing the plug to rotate if everything is timed just right.

bump key. Taking off approximately.03 inches (just shy of 1 mm) of metal from the shoulder and tip will result in a key like the one seen in Figure 4.10. This type of key can be used to perform a "push bump" technique.

The "pull" bump method

The two methods by which bumping can be performed are related, but they vary enough that separate diagrams will be used to demonstrate them. The first technique we will examine is the "pull" method. This is widely believed to be the "original" style of bumping that was popular with locksmiths for decades, long before the amateur lockpicking world and the hacker community (and, through them, the public) gained widespread knowledge of bumping.

Even though it has been cut down considerably, a bump key's blade (particularly the protruding points) will still make contact with all of the key pins in a lock as it is inserted into the keyway. With each passing stack there is a noticeable "click" that can be felt and heard. To perform a "pull" bump, the key is inserted all the way into the lock, then pulled out by "one click" (see Figure 4.11). It is then struck directly and squarely on its head, driving it into the lock. As it travels inward, the small ridge points will smash across the key pins, delivering a forceful blow to them (see Figure 4.12). Since the pins are being held in chambers and thus cannot travel laterally, the only direction in which this force can travel is "upward" towards the driver pins. The driver pins will then receive all of this energy and fly upward, leaving the plug free to rotate for a split second (see Figure 4.13).

The "push" bump method

A different type of bumping attack is possible if one us is using a key of the type shown in Figure 4.14. Known as a "push" technique, it is performed with the bump key fully inserted into the lock (see Figure 4.15). The key is not, in other words, "pulled out by one click" at the start of the procedure. The removal of extra metal near the shoulder (and tip) of the key will allow it to over-insert into the lock. This small amount of extra wiggle room is often enough to allow the small ridges of the bump key to contact the key pins and deliver adequate bumping force.

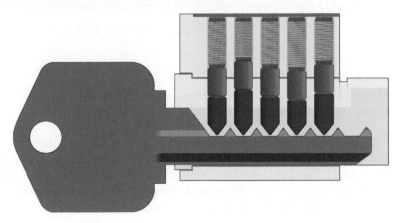

FIGURE 4.14

A "push" style bump key in position.

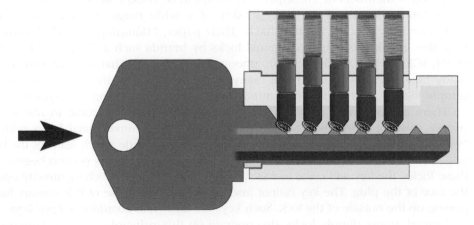

FIGURE 4.15

A "push" style bump hit being delivered.

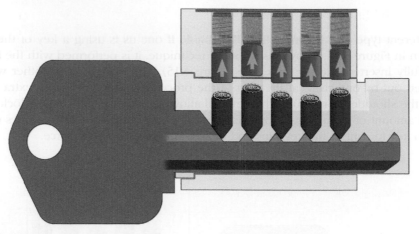

FIGURE 4.16

With the energy transferred to the driver pins, they should hopefully all jump out of position and leave the plug free to turn.

As with the "pull" method, a solid blow is delivered directly upon the rearmost protruding part of the key's head, knocking the key inward. The ridges will contact the key pins (see Figure 4.15) and the resultant force will likely be transferred up to the driver pins, thus causing them to jump out of position (Figure 4.16) so that the plug can be turned.

Tip-stopped keys

In their landmark paper on the subject of bumping, Barry Wels & Rop Gonggrijp—members of The Open Organisation of Lockpickers (TOOOL) in the Netherlands—identified the susceptibility of a wide range of locks, including higher-security models, to this attack. Their paper, "Bumping Locks," discussed how this attack was achieved against locks by brands such as Mul-T-Lock, LIPS, DOM, ICEO, Lince, and Vachette, among many others. What was interesting to many observers was the fact that many of the offerings by these companies are dimple locks… and a significant number of them operate using *tip-stopped* keys.

There are two ways in which a key for a given lock may come to rest in its proper position when inserted into the keyway. Most conventional locks with a "vertical" keyway operate using a key which has a long blade which features the bitting cuts as well as a prominent shoulder lip where the large bow portion begins. In these locks, the key will come to rest with this shoulder area touching directly upon the face of the plug. The key cannot insert any further because of this contact happening on the outside of the lock. Such keys are known as *shoulder-stopped keys*.

Indeed, many dimple locks also operate on this principle, as well. However, a significant portion of dimple locks (and many other styles of lock, as well… both high-security and basic alike) function by means of *tip-stopped keys*. These are keys where no prominent shoulder exists and no portion of the bow comes into direct contact with the lock face when the key is inserted. A tip-stopped key will ultimately settle into its proper position when the leading tip of the key contacts the deepest point within the keyway.

The members of TOOOL in the Netherlands discovered many interesting facts when researching their paper on the topic of bumping. It was apparent that the front face of a lock could become marked or dented by repeated strikes from a shoulder-stopped bump key… but even more troubling were the after-effects of using tip-stopped bump keys. The internal regions of locks that utilize tip-stopped keys were found to be less robust than the front face of most locks. Repeated blows from the leading point of a tip-stopped bump key could, they determined, lead to damage and perhaps even malfunction of the locks that one attempts to open in this manner.

Because of this, TOOOL members and their associates in the European sport-picking community began to explore ways of alleviating the internal stresses on locks being bumped. In effect, what they did in some situations was find ways to "convert" tip-stopped keys into shoulder-stopped ones. By additional modification near the bow of a key, along with the inclusion of some additional buffer material, some of our friends in Europe were able to dampen the force with which bump keys could impact a lock… transferring most of the impact to the front face and also mitigating its intensity at the same time. Two terrific examples of engineering such as this which Wels and Gonggrijp showed in their paper were the *glue stick tactic* devised by Oliver Diederichsen and the *washer tactic* pioneered by Jord Knaap. Figures 4.17 and 4.18 attempt to showcase these two methods.

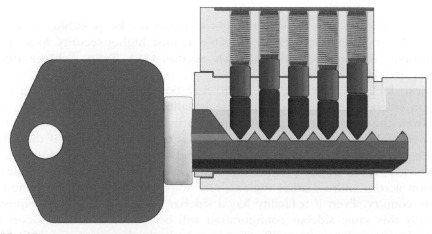

FIGURE 4.17

Here is an example of Oliver Diederichsen's "glue stick" technique for alleviating the stress normally put on a lock by a tip-stopped bump key. By trimming down the tip of the key and applying a section of glue stick near the bow, the key effectively becomes shoulder-stopped. Diederichsen would achieve this by cutting a segment of glue stick in half, then sandwiching his key blade between the pieces, heating them, and fusing the whole affair into a solid (yet slightly bouncy) mass. *NOTE: While this diagram depicts a vertical-style key blade for purposes of visual clarity, most of the time this technique is used when making bump keys for advanced dimple locks.*

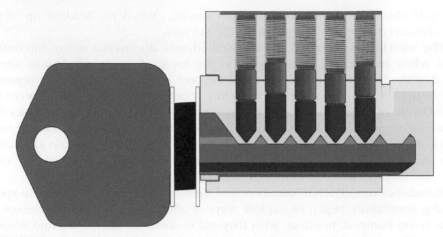

FIGURE 4.18

Here is an example of Jord Knaap's "washer" technique for alleviating the stress normally put on a lock by a tip-stopped bump key. By trimming down the tip of the key and inserting a combination of plastic washers (white) and a heavy rubber ring (black) to act as a spacer and shock absorber, Knaap could effectively make the key perform in a shoulder-stopped manner. *NOTE: While this diagram depicts a vertical-style key blade for purposes of visual clarity, most of the time this technique is used when making bump keys for advanced dimple locks.*

Sidebar mechanisms

While many individuals initially thought it would not be possible, it has been shown that bumping attacks are possible against higher-security locks which incorporate sidebar mechanisms, such as the ASSA Twin, Schlage Primus, Medeco Biaxial, and Medeco M3.

These locks, and others like them, rely both on conventional pin stacks and on sidebar mechanisms which are installed in the plug of a lock, separate from the conventional pin stacks, to provide auxiliary security. In many instances, fabricating bump keys for these locks is only feasible if the sidebar code is already known. While this may sound like an unreasonable hurdle for an attacker, it should be pointed out that some "low level" sidebar codes are uniform across entire market regions, and sometimes they are the same for a whole country. Even if a facility has a sidebar code with greater uniqueness, typically this same sidebar configuration will be shared across all doors in a master-keyed system... thus affording any authorized user of one lock in the system the ability to study and perhaps duplicate their sidebar code on to a bump key that may open other doors elsewhere in the same system.

In most of these instances, it has been my experience that sidebar mechanisms are far less tolerant of misalignment or imperfection during attempts at opening a lock. Use of a minimal-movement or negative-shoulder bump key in a "push" technique can be very problematic on certain higher-security locks which include sidebars. The Schlage Primus is one such lock.

At a TOOOL meeting in Princeton, New Jersey in 2009 multiple members were able to successfully bump open Schlage Primus locks, but only with bump keys using a "pull out" technique. The reason for this is simple… when the bump key lands its blow, the conventional pins in the lock are (hopefully) in a brief state of separation. The only way that the plug can be turned in this moment is if the sidebar is also free of any obstruction. If the bump key has comes to rest in the lock in an ideal position (a position where it normally would have been, had it been the proper key), then the sidebar will not be a problem. If, however, the key has come to rest in the lock in a *nonstandard manner* (which is the case with minimal-movement bump keys, since they will "over insert" into the lock slightly and will *not* be in an ideal position as the bump takes place), this can potentially interfere with the smooth operation of the sidebar mechanism, preventing the lock from opening.

Every situation is different, and I have seen "push" style bump keys used on ASSA Twin and Medeco Biaxial locks in the past… but more often than not I have found "pull" style bump keys to be slightly more effective against the sidebar locks encountered in commercial spaces in North America. Your best course of action is likely to be acquiring some locks from eBay or other sources and experimenting with them yourself to see how things work for you.

Remember, there are few hard-and-fast rules in physical penetration testing, beyond keeping an open mind and always seeking out whatever technique works best for *you*.

A few tips about technique

Bumping may appear to be quite a brutal tactic (and, indeed, it is not very good for the lock…it generally leaves clear indications that can be documented by forensic locksmiths and can seriously degrade the lock's functionality over time) but it is also one where some degree of finesse is necessary.

Not much thought goes into delivering the blow upon the bump key (the advice I always give to people is, simply, to try to hit the key hard enough that it will hurt if you miss) but your timing when attempting to turn the plug is critical. Some people advocate applying slight turning pressure to the key before you make your strike. While this has been known to work sometimes with the "pull" method, I personally do not recommend it. After all, any such turning force is likely to cause at least one of the pin stacks to bind, and that means at least one driver pin won't be easily able to fly upward and out of the plug.

I advise people to keep their fingers in position, near the bump key, but to not apply any turning pressure until the exact moment the hit has landed. I believe this gives you the best chance of success. In truth, it's all a matter of timing. I have seen great frustration on the faces of many people who are attempting to bump a lock...then, when it works for them one time, they suddenly cannot figure out what was so hard, and they repeat the process with success from that point on.

Having the right tool for striking the key makes some difference. Plenty of improvised bump hammers exist (I have seen everything from butter knives to screwdrivers to other locks used successfully in bumping), but some of the best tools are often purpose-built. Sadly, the one bump hammer which is the most commercially-available (developed and sold by Peterson Tools) is, in my mind, the most difficult to use. Other tools, like the legendary Tomahawk hammer and KE Mark II bump hammer, have been made in limited quantities by the leadership of TOOOL in the Netherlands and the United States, respectively, but aren't in widespread distribution.

Regarding which technique is more effective... as with most aspects of lock-picking, this varies for each individual. If I had to generalize, I would say the "pull" method might be a little bit easier to perform, but it is slower if you wish to make repeated attempts. Because the key has to be manually pulled "out" by one notch each time, an unsuccessful bump must be followed by a pause while one resets the key, then takes a position nearby with fingertips, and tries again. The "push" bump key, on the other hand, will naturally "reset" itself after every strike, allowing for repeated attempts, one after the other. I will caution you, however, that if the lock hasn't opened after a half-dozen or so blows, it is usually best to remove the key (and possibly inspect it to see if there is any noticeable damage or deformity), then re-insert it and start again.

No matter what technique is used, over time this type of attack tends to degrade the lock's internals as well as its front face. It will be quite obvious to even casual observers if a lock has been bumped repeatedly. This is particularly problematic if you are using keys made of harder materials. Many lock-opening experts advocate the creation of bump keys using material other than traditional brass. Nickel-silver or even steel bump keys are said to be more reliable and less likely to deform over time. While this may be the case, harder keys will also inevitably lead to greater damage to locks. Perhaps the best solution is some manner of hybrid design... one that incorporates hard metal keys but makes use of some of the shoulder-protecting materials like glue stick or rubber washers as described in the previous section. While that sounds like something of an interesting experiment, I doubt that I will be seen carrying such intricate bump keys in my kit any time in the near future. I will tend to stick with brass keys which have less chance of damaging a lock, and I will always keep spares in case said keys begin to show signs of wear or damage. I'd much rather have to replace my key due to a bumping attack than to replace the target lock. Bump keys also look far more innocuous on your key ring (and are less likely to be noticed at all) if they are not equipped with any such modifications.

Bump-resistant and bump-proof locks

The vast majority of pin tumbler locks in use today can be bumped open. What then, you might be wondering, makes some locks immune (or at least resistant) to this problem? There are two ways to mitigate the threat of bump key attacks. One is very expensive (and impractical for most manufacturers); the other is more achievable but is not seeing major market penetration at the time of this writing.

Certain high-security locks are outright immune to bumping either because their mechanisms do not operate with pin tumblers or because their pin stacks are augmented by additional components that wholly eliminate the risk of bumping. The following high-security locks cannot be bumped under any circumstances:

- Rotating disk locks such as those offered by Abloy and Abus
- Locks that feature "sliders" such as the EVVA 3KS
- Magnetic key systems like the EVVA MCS and many products from MIWA

This is, of course, by no means an exhaustive list. It should also be understood that most of the locks on this list retail for close to (if not more than) 100 USD. Interestingly, some locks which I would not consider high security for other reasons are, in fact, almost entirely immune to bumping attacks. Wafer locks and the "Smart Series" line by Kwikset are two such examples. I would not trust them to protect seriously sensitive areas, but you can rest assured that no one will bump these open. How, then, is bump protection achievable in typical, everyday situations where one also desires resistance to covert entry?

To address this market demand, manufacturers today are experimenting with bump-resistant pins which can be retro-fit into conventional pin tumbler locks. Two of the most successful designs to date have been pins produced by Master Lock and Ilco.

Master Lock's bumpstop technology

The Master Lock company has done extensive studies of the physics of bumping and devised a new way to prepare their lock cylinders that can often eliminate a great deal of the risk this attack poses. By changing the shape of one of their driver pins and not allowing it to drop into the plug completely (as seen in Figure 4.19) it is possible to make a bumping attempt highly impractical. With a substantial gap between the key pin and the driver pin, energy cannot transfer and the driver pin (at least in one chamber) will not move.

One aspect of Master Lock's design that makes it not 100 percent adoptable is the fact that this differently shaped driver pin has a slightly larger diameter

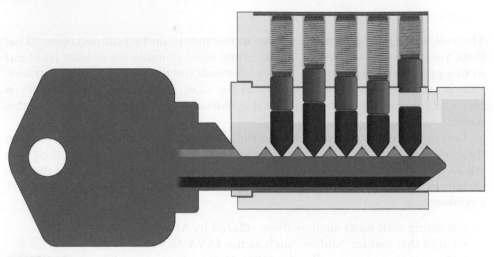

FIGURE 4.19

A lock that includes one anti-bump pin of the Master Lock BumpStop design. The driver pin in chamber #5 does not contact the key pin and thus cannot easily accept a transfer of energy during a bump attempt.

than the others in the lock. This necessitates a wider pin chamber in the housing and prevents such a pin from being installed in an aftermarket fashion.

The Ilco anti-bump pin

The Ilco company is not usually recognized as a manufacturer of locks (although they do offer a line of replacement lock cylinders) but is instead famous for being a major supplier of lock components and locksmithing supplies. Recently, they began marketing a series of pins and springs that they have designated as their "Bump Halt" solution. Instead of attempting to prevent a driver pin from dropping completely into the plug (as Master Lock does), Ilco offers locksmiths the ability to use pins of widely varying mass (along with high-strength springs) which can dramatically interfere with the physics of bumping. By installing an Ilco anti-bump driver pin (and accompanying high-strength spring) into one or two chambers (see Figure 4.20) one can drastically shift the manner in which pins behave during a bump attempt.

Because of the Ilco pin's greatly reduced mass and the higher-strength spring that sits on top of it (and, indeed, surrounds it) this pin will not travel up and down at the same speed as the other pins in the lock during a bump attempt. It is still possible to get a Bump Halt pin to jump slightly during bumping, but it is likely to have reached the crest of its leap and already be

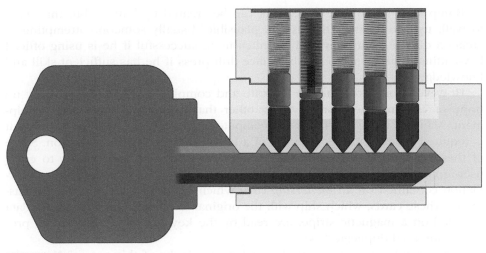

FIGURE 4.20

An Ilco Bump Halt pin and high pressure spring has been installed in the second chamber of this lock.

returning downward toward the key pin before the other "standard" driver pins have leapt up out of the plug.

My associates and I have tried installing Ilco Bump Halt pins into locks and then bumping them. I was able to successfully bump a lock with a single Ilco driver pin just once (and, as we say in lockpicking…something must be repeatable at least twice or else it doesn't count), and once we started trying locks with two such driver pins no one was able to bump the locks at all.

This is, in my view, a splendid low-cost solution to the problem of bumping. It does not eliminate the physical risk, mind you…it just makes bumping attempts incredibly unlikely to succeed. An additional benefit of this Bump Halt style of pin is that no modification to the lock's plug, housing, or key is needed. It can be retrofit into just about any pin tumbler lock with ease.

Restrictions on key cutting

Many bump keys are made by hand. While use of a proper key-cutting machine would usually be considered ideal, if you have some knowledge of the target lock and access to a hand-file, it is often possible to turn a conventional key or even a blank key into a bump key. This is particularly the case with "vertical" style keys, where cuts are made into the thin edge of the blade.

Bump keys for dimple locks, too, can be created by hand... but this starts to walk us into territory that is less plausible. Usually someone attempting to create a dimple bump key will be much more successful if he is using official key-cutting equipment (or maybe a nice drill press if he has sufficient skill and knowledge).

However, some keys are *so* intricate and complex that there is virtually no hope of creating them on anything other than original manufacturer equipment. Many of these machines are computer-controlled; no manual user input is required other than the insertion of a blank and the push of a button. Some of these machines, in the interest of security, will completely *refuse* to cut a user-input bitting code onto a key... they will *only* cut keys according to information contained on an *ownership card* which must be presented by the customer. These cards, which ship with the original lock and typically contain data encoded on a magnetic stripe, are read by the key machine and used to produce additional duplicate keys.

Is it possible, then, to create bump keys for locks of this nature? Naturally, no manufacturer is ever going to intentionally release a lock where the bitting code is 9-9-9-9-9 on all surfaces. Without a factory-original ownership card containing this data, does this mean that no bump key can ever be produced? Should a lock like this be considered bump-proof?

I would say no. Just because it is difficult to *produce* a bump key, this does not have any effect on whether or not the *mechanism within the lock itself* is susceptible to bumping. If a dedicated researcher one day discovers a way to produce a working bump key, no matter how unlikely this may be, all notions of a lock being "bump proof" become invalid.

Research of this nature is taking place even as I write this chapter. My associate Babak Javadi has developed an interest in the ownership card system used by the Mul-T-Lock company. Working with a range of sample cards from various sources, Babak has successfully reverse-engineered the encoding scheme used to store data on the magnetic stripe of the ownership cards for the new MT5 line of Mul-T-Lock products (see Figure 4.21).

Not only has Babak Javadi used magnetic-stripe software to read and decode the date on multiple lock ownership cards, but he is also able to re-write new information... creating cards that will direct key cutting machines to produce new bitting combinations that were never authorized by Mul-T-Lock. Keep an eye out for what may be an upcoming presentation at future conferences where this topic may be discussed further... there's always a chance that locks which were once thought to be secure may be shown to be susceptible to new tactics and attacks.

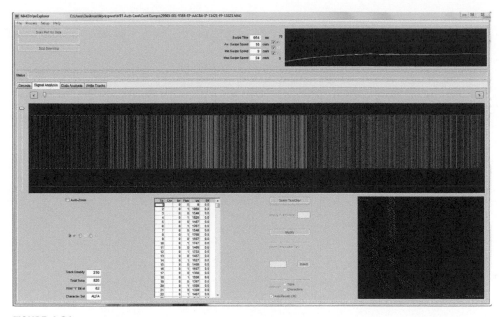

FIGURE 4.21

Screenshot from software being used to analyze the data on a multi-track magnetic stripe card.

SUMMARY

While it may not be as intricate and surreptitious a technique as impressioning or master key decoding, the use of bump keys as a way to quickly open pin tumbler locks is something that should not be dismissed in all situations. If you have the ability to make a little noise and don't mind the possibility of minor damage to the front face of a lock, a bump key may be the fastest and easiest means of ingress in certain situations.

Try bumping attacks yourself—on practice locks which you buy specifically for this purpose, of course—in order to see how effective you find them to be. My advice would be for you to acquire bump keys from a range of sources… including making your own. Give each key at least ten to twenty solid attempts before giving up, as they sometimes require a bit of a "break in" period. In the end, I suspect you will discover at least one or two bump keys that work very well for you… and which may find their way to your key ring.

Overlifting

INTRODUCTION

The term *overlifting* gets used in a number of contexts with respect to lock-picking and physical security. Before we delve into the topics contained within this chapter, a bit of disambiguation is in order.

At its core, the idea of overlifting pertains to raising or moving certain components farther than would be customary during regular operation or manipulation of a lock. I discussed this notion in at least two chapters of my first book, *Practical Lock Picking*. If a person pushes too far with one of his tools while attempting to pick a lock, a pin stack may become "over set" in a way that will interfere with the opening process (see Figure 5.1). Conversely, if someone uses a *comb pick* to intentionally lift all pin stacks to a height that is outside of their normal operating range, this can result in the easy opening of certain locks (see Figure 5.2).

This chapter will focus on a handful of very simple ways in which over-lifting tactics can be attempted using keys (blank keys are almost always the best tool for these techniques) and will showcase some of the easiest ways that locks can be opened, at least in situations where they are susceptible to such trivial attacks.

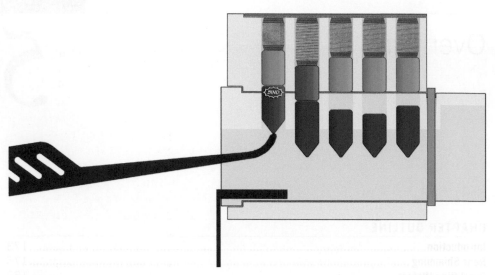

FIGURE 5.1

Accidentally pushing too far with a lockpick can raise a pin stack beyond what is desired, resulting in an "over set" pin which will interfere with the attempt at opening the lock. This unintentional occurrence is sometimes referred to as *overlifting*. This is not the style of overlifting being explored in this chapter.

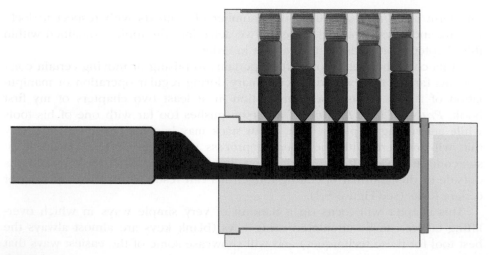

FIGURE 5.2

Using a tool such as a comb pick to raise all pin stacks simultaneously to a height outside of their normal operating range can sometimes allow the plug to turn freely, offering an adversary a very easy avenue of attack against locks susceptible to this tactic. Often this technique is described using the term *overlifting*. It is not inaccurate to use that word, but this is not the style of "overlifting" being explored in this chapter.

REAR SHIMMING

The first technique which we will discuss in our exploration of overlifting techniques is not actually used to open locked doors from the outside. However, many people will find it invaluable as a means to quickly and effectively allow the rotation—and thus the disassembly of a lock cylinder that has been removed from its housing.

As was shown during the discussion of master-keyed systems in Chapter 3, disassembly of a lock is one of the best ways to analyze and learn the top bitting codes for a large, managed infrastructure. Even locks that are *not* part of a master-keyed system can be examined internally in order to reliably produce working keys which can be used at a later date. To disassemble a lock, however, it must be open. In order to remove a plug and all of the pins one typically must use the proper key, pick open the lock, bump it, etc. In the absence of the original, working key, such manipulation techniques can be somewhat hit-or-miss and require additional time and effort. The tactic of rear shimming, however, is often a *very* reliable and easy way to free a plug in order to allow rotation and thus disassembly.

Readers of my previous work may recall my mention of *shimming* in the context of opening padlocks. Indeed, the insertion of thin pieces of metal as a means of quickly releasing a padlock's shackle is a common feature of many physical penetration testing workshops and instructional books. The activity we will discuss momentarily is also a type of "shimming" attack due to its reliance on thin metal stock and the insertion of this slim material into narrow spaces.

Locksmithing shims (often referred to as "disassembly shims" or simply "rear shims") are available from supply catalogs and are also easily fabricated from found materials. Most shims of this nature are approximately 1 inch long and ¼ inches wide, and are found in thicknesses ranging from 0.0015 inches to 0.0030 inches. A photograph of a pin tumbler lock core and two rear-side shims can be seen in Figure 5.3.

TIP

The most popular sources for improvising locksmithing rear-side shims are acousto-magnetic anti-theft tags which interact with retail loss-prevention equipment operating in the 58 kHz range. These small tags can typically be found inside CD and DVD cases. If you split open these small plastic tags, it is often possible to extract small pieces of metal (a magnetostrictive strip and a bias magnet strip, if you are technically curious) which will work quite well as rear-shims.

In addition to a small piece of shim metal, the other tool necessary for rear shimming is a blank key. Insert the blank key into the lock you wish to disassemble. This will lift all of the pin stacks so that the shear line between all key pins and driver pins is "above" the edge of the plug in every pin stack (see Figure 5.4). The shim metal will be inserted from the rear side of the lock

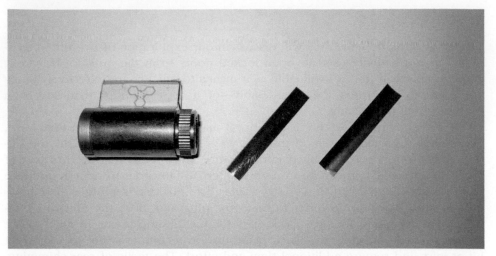

FIGURE 5.3

The opening of this lock by means of rear shimming will be shown in the coming photographs and diagrams. Only one of the two shims pictured here will be required.

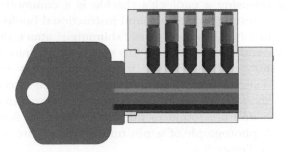

FIGURE 5.4

A blank key is used to lift all pin stacks. The locksmithing shim cannot be inserted yet, because of the presence of a tail assembly on the rear of the plug. In these diagrams and photos, that tail assembly takes the form of a screw-cap. It will have to be removed before the process of shimming can be started.

core, but as Figure 5.4 shows, the presence of any tail clip or tail ring will inter-fere with this process.

Plug retaining mechanisms and tail pieces come in many shapes and sizes, but detaching them tends to be a relatively straightforward process. Sometimes small screws are removed in order to free a cam plate. Other times a snap-ring will have to be released with the assistance of small tools such as needle-nose pliers. In these photographs and diagrams, a screw cap is shown. It is seen removed in Figure 5.5, by means of depressing a small spring-loaded plunger in order to allow counter-clockwise rotation of the cap.

With the blank key in the lock, slip the shim along the "top" of the plug where it protrudes from the rear of the housing (see Figure 5.6). It will not be

FIGURE 5.5

Here we see the lock core with its tail piece removed. The screw cap has been taken off and we are now ready to insert the blank key in the front side and the disassembly shim in the rear side.

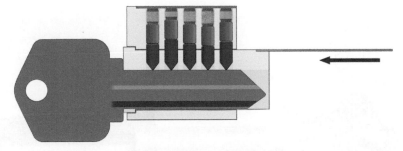

FIGURE 5.6

With the blank key in place, the shim is inserted along the "top" edge of the plug. *As has been noted elsewhere in this book, I am displeased at having to use such culturally-biased descriptor words as "top" and "bottom" when discussing pin tumbler locks... however, sometimes for purposes of clarity one must simply avoid ambiguity. In all of the examples in this chapter, locks are depicted and described from a North American perspective where pin stacks typically rest "on top" of the key. In many European installations, locks are mounted in a reverse fashion, with pins and the bulk of the housing "below" the plug. The physics relevant to these techniques will apply in either case, however.*

possible to insert the shim particularly deep into the lock at this time, since it will make contact with a pin stack (see Figures 5.7 and 5.8).

The next step in the process of rear shimming involves slowly retracting the blank key—in order to allow the deep most pin stack to "drop down" slowly—while maintaining gentle pressure on the shim. By attempting to insert the shim deeper into the lock as the pin stack is moving, it is often possible to slide the shim in between the key pin and the driver pin (see Figure 5.9). Sometimes more than one attempt is required (this is trivial, since the blank key can be repeatedly inserted and removed as often as is necessary) but usually the process is simple. The only real difficulties one may encounter are situations when the key pins have odd shapes and are not perfectly cylindrical.

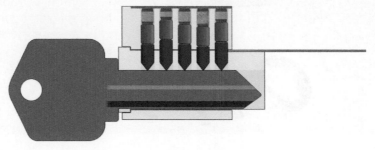

FIGURE 5.7
The shim cannot be inserted particularly far into the lock, because it will butt up against the key pin in the deep most position (in these diagrams, that would be the key pin in the #5 position).

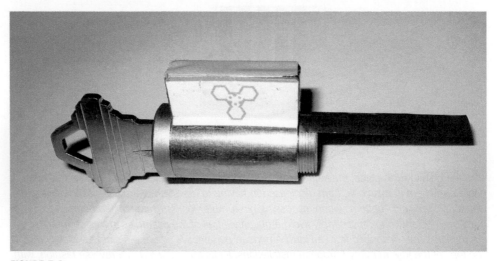

FIGURE 5.8
Here is a photo showing the shim inserted as far as is possible at first.

TIP

The two types of non-standard key pins which you might encounter are serrated pins and torpedo pins. Readers of my previous book (*Practical Lock Picking*) may recall mention of serrated pins in Chapter 4. Serrations, when they appear, tend to be a feature of driver pins... but some manufacturers (such as American Lock, a brand that has been acquired by the Master Lock company) have been known to incorporate serrations on key pins, as well. Torpedo-shaped key pins, which are used to prevent impressioning, are even less common than serrated key pins... featured only occasionally in some higher-security offerings such as locks produced by the ASSA company.

While serrated or torpedo key pins can occasionally make rear shimming difficult, it is far from impossible, even on locks where they are present. I am unaware of any manufacturer of locks that produces or uses pins which are specifically designed to frustrate rear shimming.

Each pin stack can be handled in the same way. As you withdraw the blank key, continue inserting the shim deeper into the lock (see Figure 5.10). Ultimately, if you are successful, it should be possible to separate the key pins and driver pins of every single pin stack (see Figures 5.11 and 5.12) and then remove the key completely, as shown in Figure 5.13.

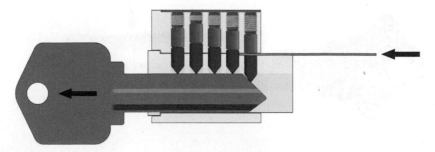

FIGURE 5.9

It is possible to use the leading edge of the key blade to raise or lower pin stacks in order to slide the shim material in between the key pin and the driver pin.

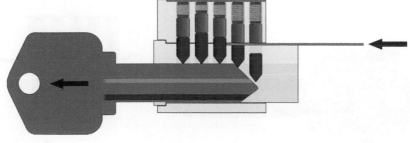

FIGURE 5.10

Rear shimming proceeds with the blank key being slowly removed while the shim is continually inserted farther into the lock from the tail side of the plug.

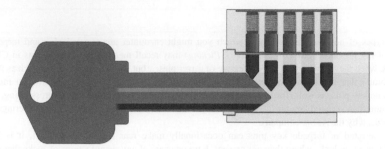

FIGURE 5.11

Eventually, the shim can be worked all the way through the lock, separating each pin stack and keeping the driver pins out of the plug in every position.

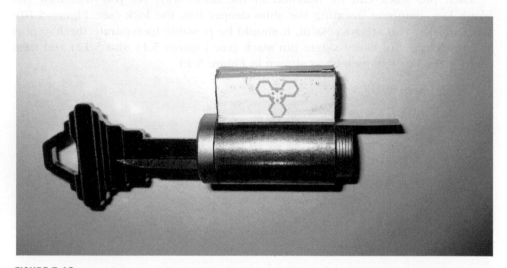

FIGURE 5.12

Here we see a photograph of a lock that has been successfully shimmed from the rear.

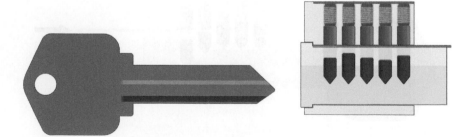

FIGURE 5.13

Once shimming is complete, you can remove the blank key entirely.

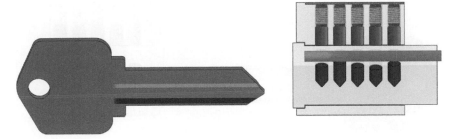

FIGURE 5.14

With no pins in the way anymore, the plug can be turned. The blank key shown in these diagrams is also pictured as being slightly turned, simply to help with perspective.

FIGURE 5.15

This lock has been successfully shimmed from the tail side and the plug is now turned.

With the shim metal holding the driver pins "up" in the housing, the plug can be turned. As shown in Figures 5.14 and 5.15, it is perfectly fine for the shim metal to move with the plug during rotation. The driver pins will stay in their lifted position once the plug has turned. You can even remove the shim material entirely if you wish (see Figure 5.16).

With the lock successfully turned and the tail piece already removed, you could now disassemble the lock if you desire. Be sure to do so carefully, possibly with the aid of a follower tool, if it is your intention to analyze the pinning configuration and decode the bitting of the keys which operate the lock.

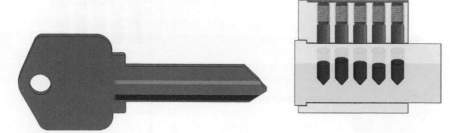

FIGURE 5.16

Once the plug has been turned, there is no reason that the shim must be kept in place. It can be removed entirely if you wish.

OVERLIFTING WAFERS

The preceding section described a tactic that is available to you if a lock cylinder has been removed from a door or padlock, but that technique is not viable against a lock in the field. However, a different method of employing overlifting *can* be used to attack locks which are installed and in use. First we will explore how this can be performed on wafer locks; later we will examine the same style of tactic being used against pin tumbler locks.

In its most basic form, overlifting as a means of opening a lock involves raising all internal components up and then interfering with the manner in which they "fall" back down again. If this is performed correctly against a susceptible lock, the wafers or pins on the inside will *not* fall back to their original, default position... the idea is to get them "caught" in such a way that they will stay at the edge of the plug, ultimately allowing it to turn.

One style of lock that has been popular at TOOOL demonstrations is the AXA bicycle lock seen in Figure 5.17. Popular in the homeland of our Dutch friends, this is a product designed for mounting on a bike's frame in order to lock the rear wheel if the retaining bar is engaged in the closed position.

Readers of my previous book will recall that wafer locks function in a manner very similar to pin tumbler locks, with metal components that can either block or allow the rotation of a plug, depending on the degree to which they are lifted up by the blade of a key. Figure 5.18 shows generic diagrams of a wafer lock, from both front-facing and side-view perspectives.

> **NOTE**
>
> For purposes of clarity, the next five diagrams omit a visual depiction of the blank key in the lock. Please refer to the captions and associated text for descriptions of when the blank key is used and when it is removed.

If a blank key is inserted into this style of lock, all of the wafers within will be raised considerably (see Figure 5.19). If turning pressure is then applied to

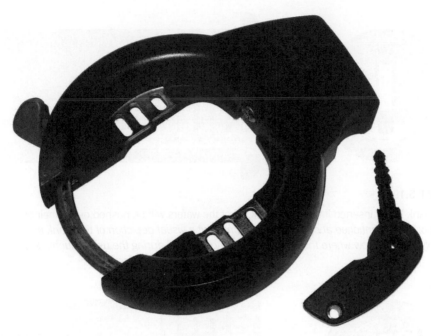

FIGURE 5.17

This AXA brand bike lock uses a wafer mechanism that is susceptible to an overlifting attack.

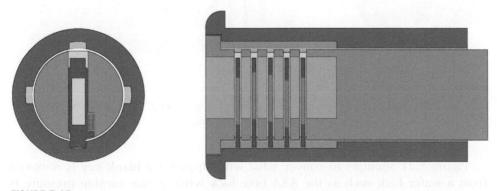

FIGURE 5.18

These images represent a basic wafer lock, shown from both a front- and side-view perspective. The lock and plug are shown in gray; the wafers are seen in a hue that represents their brass construction, as this is the most typical metal used for that purpose.

said key, it can be possible to push the plug slightly out of alignment within its housing, as shown in Figure 5.20. While this is not going to allow the plug to turn, it can have ramifications in terms of how these wafers will fall back down as the key is slowly removed.

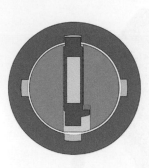

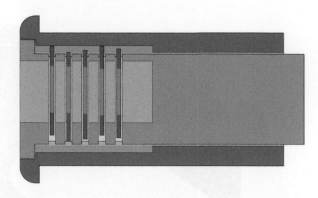

FIGURE 5.19

If a blank key is inserted into a wafer lock, all of the wafers will be pushed out of their original positions. *As mentioned above, these diagrams omit a visual depiction of the blank key itself, and simply seek to show where the wafers would be positioned during the use of such a key.*

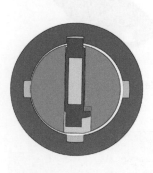

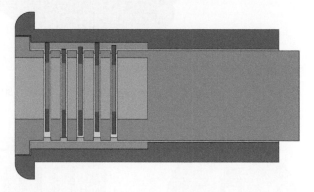

FIGURE 5.20

If turning pressure is applied to the lock while a blank key is inserted, the plug can be pushed slightly out of alignment and will be off-center in the housing.

Figure 5.21 attempts to convey what will happen if a blank key is removed from a wafer lock such as the AXA bike lock while gentle turning pressure is being applied to the plug. Figure 5.22 shows this in greater detail. Because of the subtle angle at which the plug and the wafers are canted (because turning force has been applied to the plug) they will not fall back to their original position (binding below the plug) but instead will catch on the lip of the housing. If all wafers catch in this manner, the plug will not be held static and can be turned just as though the proper key were being used (see Figure 5.23).

We have performed this demonstration many times at security conferences, schools, and other educational events. When the loud snapping sound of the AXA lock popping open is heard, the audience never ceases to be amazed, given that the lock has operated with a blank nearly as easily as it would have

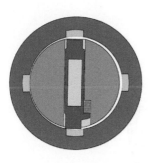
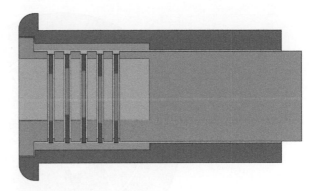

FIGURE 5.21

With the plug in an off-center position, removal of the blank key will often result in the wafers failing to fall completely back down to their original position… they can become "stuck" on the lip of the housing as they drop.

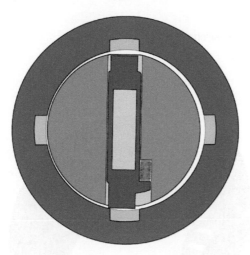

FIGURE 5.22

This enlarged diagram seeks to show in greater detail how a wafer can become "stuck" on the edge of the housing as it drops when the blank key is removed. Now this wafer is no longer binding above or below the plug.

with the original key (see Figure 5.24). A video showing this attack being performed is available on the web site associated with this book.

WARNING

Any time you attempt to cause a lock to operate improperly or you bind components in an effort to make them come to rest in non-standard positions, you run the risk of damaging the lock. Overlifting attacks against wafer locks can cause stuck keys, failure to open, or break the lock entirely if they are attempted in a less than graceful way. If something isn't working for you, don't force it.

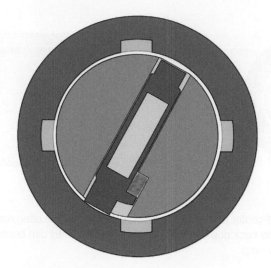

FIGURE 5.23

If no wafers are in binding positions, the plug can turn freely.

FIGURE 5.24

The AXA lock has been opened by a blank key due to the over-lifting of the wafers within.

Many wafer locks use mechanisms with double-sided keys, in which some wafers are installed in the "top" of the plug and others are installed in the "bottom" resulting in varied binding from both sides when the lock is at rest. While it may be more difficult to perform an overlifting attack such as this against a lock like that, it is not impossible. The best means of preventing overlifting attacks against wafer locks is to machine the components to tighter tolerances during production.

OVERLIFTING PINS

At times overlifting techniques such as the one discussed in the preceding section are possible against pin tumbler locks. In general, these styles of locks do not feature tolerances of a sufficiently sloppy nature to perform this attack. However, at times certain locks are susceptible because of oversights or outright errors during production.

Years ago, the noted lock collector and researcher Han Fey presented me with a unique gift. It was a lock that had been incorrectly produced using pins of a wrong diameter. While the driver pins (which usually hold the lock shut) were of the appropriate size, the key pins were marginally too small, as can be seen in Figure 5.25.

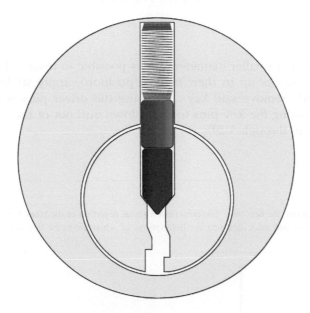

FIGURE 5.25

If manufacturers are not careful in their fabrication and assembly of products, situations like this can arise. Note how the red key pin has a smaller diameter than the blue driver pin. This would never be intentional.

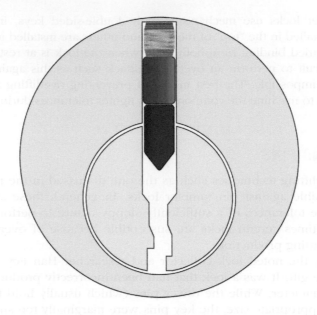

FIGURE 5.26

Overlifting the pin stacks in a lock with this type of design flaw can lead to a simple exploit. Here we see the pins raised up by means of inserting a blank key.

Because of their smaller diameter, it was possible to insert a blank key (thus raising the pin stacks up to their highest position), apply slight turning pressure, and slowly remove said key… catching the driver pins at the top of the plug while allowing the key pins to drop down and out of the way completely (see Figures 5.26 through 5.29).

NOTE

For purposes of clarity, the next three diagrams omit a visual depiction of the blank key in the lock. Please refer to the captions and associated text for descriptions of when the blank key is used and when it is removed.

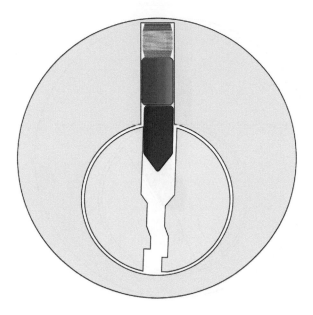

FIGURE 5.27

Application of slight turning pressure to the key will cause the driver pin to stick farther out to the side.

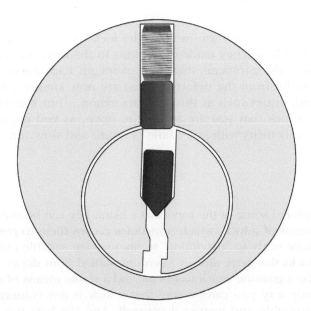

FIGURE 5.28

If the blank key (which is not shown, as per the earlier note) is slowly removed with slight turning pressure being maintained the whole time, the driver pins will tend to "catch" on the edge of the plug instead of falling back down to their default positions.

FIGURE 5.29

With the driver pins stuck outside of the plug, nothing is binding and the plug can turn freely, allowing the lock to open. A video showing this attack is available on the web site associated with this book.

Han Fey was quick to inform me that the lock's vendor had identified this manufacturing problem. They made corrections to their production process and sought to address the problems that their oversight had created. These locks (the ones that suffer from the defective pins) are now simply collectors' items. In the real world, errors such as this are uncommon... but it never hurts to try a blank key in a lock that you are seeking to open, as you might be very surprised if it suddenly turns with just a little pressure and slow removal process!

SUMMARY

This chapter explored some of the ways that a blank key can be used to lift up the internal components of a lock, which sometimes causes them to perform in unexpected ways. Some of these "overlifting" techniques are suitable only as means of disassembling locks that have already been uninstalled from doors; at other times overlifting can be a genuine attack technique and a viable means of opening locks.

Often the only way you can be sure that a lock is not vulnerable to such a tactic is to disassemble and inspect it yourself. And the best way to determine if a lock in the field is susceptible tends to be acquiring a blank key and simply seeing how the lock behaves. Test the locks upon which you rely, and probe the locks you wish to open. Overlifting has a habit of popping up and being possible in the most unexpected places.

Skeleton Keys

6

CHAPTER OUTLINE

INTRODUCTION

I have a confession to make. No matter how transparent the characters or how trite the subject matter, I enjoy James Bond films. Ever since I was little (I cannot now recall if *The Spy Who Loved Me* or *Octopussy* was the first 007 film I viewed in a theater) I have enjoyed the thrilling action sequences, exotic locales... and, of course, the gadgets produced by the MI6 engineers of Q Branch. The 1987 Bond film *The Living Daylights* still resonates with me in terms of the secret agent's assorted equipment. I remember watching Desmond Llewelyn's character displaying a key to James Bond, remarking that it would be able to "open 90 percent of the world's locks" (see Figure 6.1). You can have your fantasies of a heavily-armed, outrigger-enabled, laser-equipped, and rocket-boosted Aston Martin[1]... but I was in awe of the simplicity and beauty of a small key that could open an almost infinite number of doors.

---

[1]I should point out that if any of my readers do have the desire to surprise me with an Aston Martin V8 Vantage featuring such trappings—or any DB5 or V12 Vanquish, even without such armament or gadgetry—I will by no means turn down such a gift.

FIGURE 6.1

Here we see Major Geoffrey Boothroyd a.k.a. "Q" portrayed by Desmond Llewelyn in the 1987 film *The Living Daylights* as he presents James Bond with a key that can allegedly open the vast majority of the world's locks. Unfortunately, such a key does not exist outside of Hollywood but the concept is quite appealing and germane to this chapter.

While keys like the ones seen in modern secret agent fiction may be complete fantasy, throughout history there have been special keys affording the ability to bypass the security within certain locks. The ability to open many locks in ways that manufacturers did not intend is often achieved by removing material from keys. Cutting away all "extra flesh" in the metal, if you will, results in only the most basic and essential "bones" left behind when you are done. Because of this, devices made by filing or cutting material from keys until only the minimal useful components remain are known as *skeleton keys*.

Skeleton keys are most often used in *warded locks* although versions of these keys have historically been used in other types of hardware, as well. In the past, skeleton keys were seen attacking *lever locks* (also sometimes referred to as Chubb locks). Most lever locks produced today (they are still quite popular in England, around the Mediterranean, and in South America; they are far less common in the United States) are more modern and not as susceptible to such trivial attack. However, warded locks—despite being similarly archaic in their overall design—are still regularly sold and used in North America. Although they offer virtually no security due to their unsophisticated internal mechanisms, you can still find warded locks in virtually every hardware store in the United States.

This chapter will examine how skeleton keys (as well as warded picks, which function in the exact same manner) operate and how you can best use them in order to attack warded locks.

WARDED LOCKS

Some of the most affordable and best-selling kinds of padlocks sold in big-box hardware stores such as Home Depot tend to be the Model #22 and Model #500 products from Master Lock. Despite functioning by means of a design that has remained relatively unchanged since ancient times (warded locks were actually being criticized for their weak security as far back as the 18th and 19th centuries!) these locks remain popular among people seeking very cheap hardware that can be used in harsh conditions. In particular, the models within the 500-series family which feature a *breakaway shackle* (one that is completely removed from the lock body when the lock is opened) are a mainstay of storage sheds, perimeter fences, and other applications where the lock is likely to be exposed to environmental conditions and dirt or fouling.

Photos of these popular warded locks—which are still produced and sold today—are seen in Figures 6.2 and 6.3. Note the jagged "lightning bolt" keyway profile seen in Figure 6.3… that is always a sure-fire way to identify a warded lock in the field.

Let's take a closer look at how warded locks such as these function. Figure 6.4 shows a diagram of a typical warded key, and Figure 6.5 shows

FIGURE 6.2

Here we see Master Lock #22 and #500 padlocks, along with one of their keys. They are both warded locks. The key substantiates this fact with its highly right-angled bitting cuts. Unlike the blade of a key designed for a pin-tumbler or wafer lock (where internal components ride along gentle slopes) a warded lock's key does not have to be smooth. Because these locks rarely contain any active components (most warded locks operate using only a spring-powered latch) no surface of the key makes contact with anything of substance while it is being inserted. It is only when the key begins to *turn* that it will touch other parts of the lock. This will become clear momentarily.

FIGURE 6.3

Even if a key were not available for visual inspection, both of these padlocks are instantly recognizable as being warded locks. The distinct "lightning bolt"-shaped keyway is always a clear giveaway of this fact.

FIGURE 6.4

A key for a warded lock. It features a distinct blade, a bow/head, bitting cuts, and so on. All of these are features of keys that we have seen before… but warded locks are considerably different.

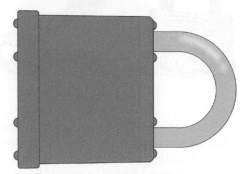

FIGURE 6.5

From the outside, a warded lock does not often appear all that distinct from other locks you may have seen. Like all padlocks, there is a shackle, a keyway, etc. As we are about to see, however, on the inside the similarities to pin tumbler mechanisms end.

the customary outer appearance of an average warded lock. From the outside, an untrained observer might not think these locks function in a manner that is substantially different from the items we have already discussed in this book. After all, like conventional pin tumbler locks, these products feature keys with bitting cuts, a keyway with what might appear to be a round plug that turns when the lock is operated, a notched shackle retained by an internal bolt or latch mechanism of some kind... how distinct could warded locks really be?

Let's look inside

While pin tumbler locks (and even wafer locks) have a variety of internal components that interact with every bit of the key, warded locks offer no such sophistication. Internally, most warded locks contain only a latch mechanism holding the shackle in place (see Figure 6.6). All of the cuts and bits of protruding metal that are seen on the blades of their keys may look impressive, but most of those bits perform no real function... other than to *prevent* the key from being used in the *wrong* lock. Figures 6.7 through 6.10 attempt to convey what is happening when the lock is opened.

Figure 6.10 shows how the lock is able to open easily once the small red latch has been pulled back and out of the way. Naturally, in addition to the spring-assist mechanism which helps to pop the lock open, the inner end of the shackle would feature some additional flange or thicker diameter (not pictured) so as to prevent it from falling completely out of the lock body.

The only exception to this would be padlocks featuring what are known as "break free" shackles, which are specifically designed to be removed completely when the lock is open.

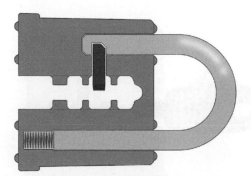

FIGURE 6.6

While there is a fair bit of machining and protruding points of metal (these are the "wards" from which this style of lock takes its name), internally this lock is particularly simple. The only mechanism that keeps the lock closed is a spring loaded latch (seen in red; for purposes of clarity and to avoid clutter the spring is not depicted in this diagram) that holds the shackle in place.

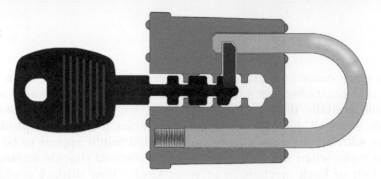

FIGURE 6.7

This diagram represents the warded key being inserted into the padlock. I hope this visually conveys to you how, within the keyway, the wards themselves are off to the side slightly. The "wider" portions of the key can pass by the wards while it is being inserted, but they will prevent the *wrong* key from *turning* in the lock, as will be seen in Figure 6.12.

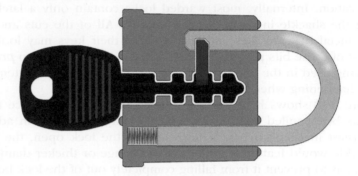

FIGURE 6.8

The key is now totally inserted into the lock (although this diagram does not convey it completely, most warded keys are *tip stopped* as opposed to *shoulder stopped*). Since the wider bits on the key are aligned perfectly with the gaps in between any wards inside of the lock body, this key would be able to turn in its current position.

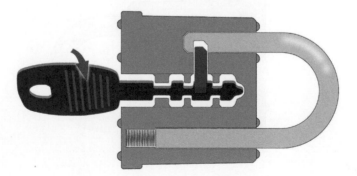

FIGURE 6.9

With the key in the lock one bit on the blade will be aligned with the latch mechanism. When the user begins to turn the key, this bit will hook against this latch and start to retract it.

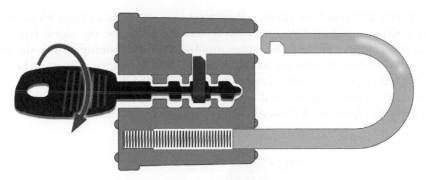

FIGURE 6.10

Here we see the warded key has completely turned (almost a full 180 degrees) and the latch mechanism has been retracted enough to allow the shackle to release.

TIP

If you have ever encountered warded locks with break free shackles (like many of the Master Lock #500 products seen on store shelves), you may have noticed that there are notches running down *both* sides of these shackles. This sort of design leads some people to assume that the lock itself features at least two latch mechanisms… one for each side of the shackle.

This is not the case. Nowadays almost all of the basic warded locks that you can find in hardware stores feature only a single internal latch, such as those depicted in the preceding diagrams. Shimming is usually possible (shimming attacks were described in Chapter 5 of my earlier work, *Practical Lock Picking*) by means of inserting metal into only one side of these locks.

Then why are the notches machined down both sides of the shackle? It is simply a convenience for users so that they may secure the lock by re-attaching the body mechanism in either direction.

WARNING

On padlocks with break free shackles, users may re-secure a lock by inserting the shackle's loose ends into either hole in the lock body… but this does *not* mean they are free to throw caution completely to the wind.

One does need to re-close the padlock *with the keyway facing out, away from the shackle itself*. Although the shape of the internal components makes it rather difficult, *it is possible to accidentally re-secure the lock body in an "upside down" fashion*. Doing so will totally obscure and block access to the keyway, preventing the lock from being removed with the key or even with pick tools. Locks that have been improperly secured in this manner can be opened with shims, but it can be a difficult and frustrating prospect.

It's a far better plan to take care when closing a padlock like this… just because the shackle is designed for user convenience does not mean you can disregard caution entirely.

Where's the security?

So how, then, do locks of such simple design provide any security at all? Modern warded locks attempt to provide some degree of protection by introducing variations in the size and spacing of the bits on the blade of each key. Go to your local hardware store and examine a few warded locks on the shelves. (Or just purchase them… they tend to cost no more than $5 or $6 USD apiece.) Compare their keys. It is likely that they will be the same length and width, with approximately the same number of bits running down the blade. The only distinctions you are likely to notice will be minor. Figure 6.11 shows two warded keys… see how closely they resemble each other?

Imagine trying to insert and turn this alternate key into the lock we have already seen. Figure 6.12 shows how well that would work.

FIGURE 6.11

A comparison of two warded keys. The top key is the one we saw in previous diagrams. The bottom key is ostensibly one that would operate a different lock. Notice how few differences there are between them. Also notice that they each seem to share a "sweet spot" approximately one-quarter of the way in from the tip. The importance of this will be revealed shortly.

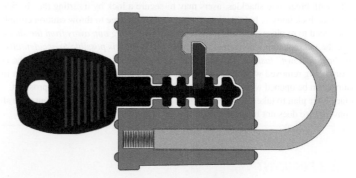

FIGURE 6.12

It is possible to *insert* an improper key into a warded lock of the same type. But because the bits on the key do not match with the wards and gaps within the lock body, this key will not be able to *turn* and therefore will not be able to engage the latch mechanism.

SIMPLE SKELETON KEYS

As you can see in Figure 6.12, a key should not be able to turn inside the "wrong" warded lock. However, what *exactly* is preventing this key from turning? Is it the wards within the lock body? Is it the shape of the key? In actuality, it is *the conjunction* of these two features… when they are mismatched the key will not operate the lock.

However, consider this… is the *entirety* of the key a crucial part of this lock's functionality? Just how much of the key is truly needed in order to make this lock operate? Naturally, the portion of the key that engages the latch mechanism is necessary. But what about all of the other bits on the key… are they crucial to the lock in any way? If you were to remove all of the other portions of the key, save for the bit that actually touches the latch mechanism, you would have a skeleton key (see Figure 6.13).

If this key were to be inserted into the same padlock we've seen thus far, it should operate the lock without any difficulty (see Figure 6.14). The critical

FIGURE 6.13

By removing all of the "extra flesh" on a warded key, one is left only with the "bare bones" necessary to open a lock. Hence, a key such as this one is popularly known as a *skeleton key.*

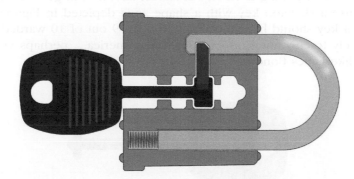

FIGURE 6.14

This key will still function just fine within the lock. The part that is necessary for operation remains; the parts which serve only to *disallow* use of this key in other locks are gone. This key will still work in this lock… and will now most likely work in *almost all other locks* of the same make and model.

component on the key still remains, and all the superfluous parts are removed. However, as many of you may realize… it should now be possible to use this key in *almost any* warded lock from this family of products.

Because most of the keys from this manufacturer (at least within this model line of padlocks) tend to have their "sweet spot" in the same location, filing down all except this portion of the key will often allow you to open every single one of these locks.

A more universal skeleton key

Of course, it is entirely possible that warded locks of other models or different brands might have their "sweet spot" in a different position on their keys. Indeed, it is common for various warded locks to have their operating latch at a different depth inside the lock body. It is for this reason that most people who remove metal in the hopes of making a skeleton key choose to produce something akin to what can be seen in Figure 6.15. With a thinner bit of metal, farther out to the tip of the key, this will be more likely to turn successfully in a wider range of warded locks.

TIP

While a skeleton key created in this manner (by removing all material except the bitting at the very tip) will tend to function in a wider range of locks, it does lose its capability to automatically self-center in the correct position when being inserted into a padlock (see Figure 6.16). A skeleton key such as this offers the user greater flexibility, but typically it is necessary to move the key back and forth in the keyway a bit, retracting it until the tip can be felt hitting the latch mechanism within (see Figure 6.17).

It takes a bit of getting used to, but almost anyone can get the hang of how it feels to use a skeleton key with a shape as is depicted in Figures 6.16 and 6.17. Such a key should have the ability to open 9 out of 10 warded locks that you are likely to encounter, at least in North America… perhaps you may yet get to feel like James Bond!

FIGURE 6.15

This is the most common modification of a warded key. By removing all of the metal except for the bit at the very tip, this key is likely to function in a wider range of locks. If the tip-most bit on a stock key is particularly thick, during this filing process it is usually modified to be thinner.

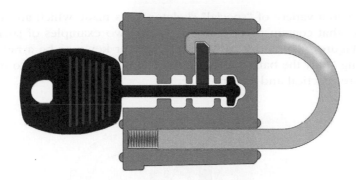

FIGURE 6.16

A skeleton key which has cbeen produced in a way that makes it highly universal is unlikely to align perfectly in the correct position by simply being inserted into a lock. Often, the functional bit that remains on such a key will not be aligned with the latch mechanism.

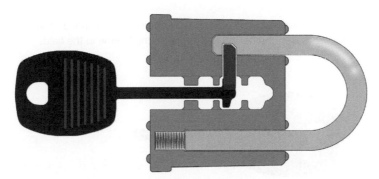

FIGURE 6.17

In order to open a warded lock with a highly universal skeleton key, it is often necessary to pull the key slightly "out" of the lock in an attempt to find the latch mechanism. Once you have located the right position, it is sometimes difficult to hold the key steady as you turn it (since the key now lacks all of the other bits that used to interact with wards in order to help the key to remain centered) but it should open the lock.

MORE COMPLICATED SKELETON KEYS

Very occasionally, I have encountered warded locks in the field that operate using more than one internal latch mechanism (see Figure 6.18). Almost all of the times this has happened, the lock has been rather old and appeared to be well-worn. I do not recall encountering a brand new warded lock on store shelves recently which featured more than one latch.

I have seen a variety of "special" skeleton keys made which are designed to attack locks that contain more than one latch. Two examples of such keys are shown in Figures 6.19 and 6.20. While the former key may be a rather elegant way of using "only the bare minimum of metal necessary" I tend to find the latter key more practical and easier to use.

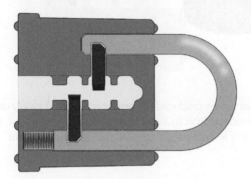

FIGURE 6.18

Some warded locks have more than one latching mechanism. This is not as common on locks produced and sold nowadays, but they do appear from time to time in the field.

FIGURE 6.19

This is one modification designed to produce a skeleton key that will operate a warded lock containing two latches. I have never personally seen anyone keep this style of key in their toolkit.

FIGURE 6.20

This is a more typical way to produce a skeleton key for opening warded locks with two latches. It has worked well most of the time, in my experience.

WARDED PICKS

Some of you may have seen tools in locksmithing catalogs that look very similar to the keys seen in Figures 6.15 and 6.20. How many of you have come across picks which appear like the one seen in Figure 6.21? Do you see the similarity between this and what we have already examined?

Tools like this are known simply as *warded picks.* Perhaps we're being a bit generous with the title of "pick" in this instance... since very little finesse or light touch is involved with these items. They are really nothing more than skeleton keys fabricated using thinner metal stock. The notion is that by manufacturing them from flatter metal, they can be inserted into warded locks with varying keyways (not all warded locks have that distinctive "lightning bolt" keyway, after all).

Warded picks are often sold in kits. The five most typical tools in such collections are seen in Figure 6.22. I have encountered warded tools being

FIGURE 6.21

Notice how similar this tool is to the skeleton key seen in Figure 6.20.

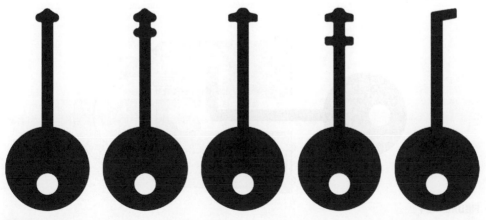

FIGURE 6.22

These are the most typical shapes for warded picks that one finds for sale in catalogs and on the internet.

produced by many manufacturers and being sold in a wide variety of catalogs… yet they all seem to offer these same exact five tools: a small single and small double pick, a large single and large double pick, and a one-sided pick which is popularly known as a "hockey stick" design.

As shown in Figures 6.23 and 6.24, it is often possible to use more than one style of warded pick in a given lock. As long as you can reach the latch mechanism(s) and get it to release, the lock should open. Indeed, it is often possible to use "double" picks in locks that contain only one latch (see Figure 6.25). I have found that in many cases this actually helps to stabilize and center the pick tool more easily.

Conversely, it is also possible to use "single" picks in warded locks that feature more than one latch. Because these latch mechanisms interact with the shackle directly (as opposed to one degree of separation like what is seen in

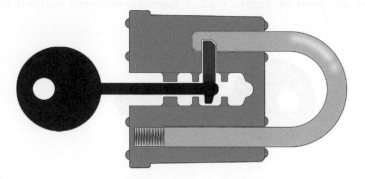

FIGURE 6.23

Here we see a typical warded pick (the same one shown in Figure 6.21) reaching the latch inside a warded lock.

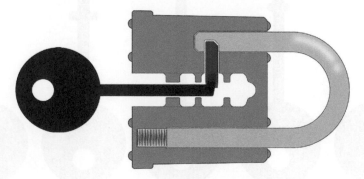

FIGURE 6.24

Here we see another warded pick (the style popularly known as a "hockey stick" shape) reaching the latch inside a warded lock.

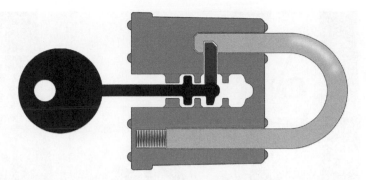

FIGURE 6.25

Even though this warded lock has only one latch, it is possible to use a "double" pick and open it easily.

pin tumbler locks, where alignment of the pins allows the *plug* to turn, and only then does this trigger a different mechanism allowing the lock or door to open) it is often possible to apply considerable "pulling" pressure on the lock and hunt around within by using your warded pick. You can usually cause one latch to catch prematurely and, by continuing to pull on the lock body, you can then "bind" said latch in an open position. Then when you find and retract the other latch the lock will open.

WARNING

While it is often possible to attempt to open a warded lock using most or even all of the items in a warded pick kit, I must advise you that the best course of action is to *start small*. Try the narrower pick tools in your kit first. If these do not work, explore around inside with the "hockey stick" pick for a bit. Only then, if the lock still does not want to open after repeated attempts, is it advisable to try the "wider" tools.

It is absolutely possible to get warded picks permanently stuck inside of a lock. This happens when attempting to use a tool which is too wide. I have witnessed picks like this jammed in locks four distinct times in the past… I have *never* seen them successfully removed without destroying the lock in the process. If you are attempting to be surreptitious in your actions, getting a tool stuck inside a lock is not something you wish to have happen on a penetration job.

TYPES OF WARDED LOCKS

While it is tempting to think of all warded locks as being exactly the same inside, they do appear with some variety in the real world. Most warded locks being *sold* today show little diversity, but because of their incredible capability to resist weathering and environmental damage (this is a natural byproduct of their very simplistic construction and lack of intricate internal components) it is very common to encounter warded locks that have been in use for decades.

FIGURE 6.26

A typical warded lock that I encountered on a penetration test. It was in an outdoor location, protecting the entire building's power supply.

Warded locks are most often found in outdoor locations (see Figure 6.26). Because of their resistance to rain, ice, mud, dirt, sand, corrosion, and other problems that can cause different styles of locks to become inoperable, it is normal to see warded locks on power panels, utility boxes, outdoor sheds, fence gates, and so forth.

As was mentioned at the beginning of this chapter, the most popular models of warded locks sold today tend to feature a distinct "lightning bolt" keyway (see Figure 6.27). Interestingly, this keyway comes in two forms, with one being a direct mirror of the other. This makes skeleton keys harder to use than purely flat warded picks.

I have also encountered warded locks that are entirely one-sided, even with keys that feature bitting cuts which are not symmetrical (see Figure 6.28). However, these have all been exceedingly old locks... I have not found such a lock for sale on store shelves in recent years.

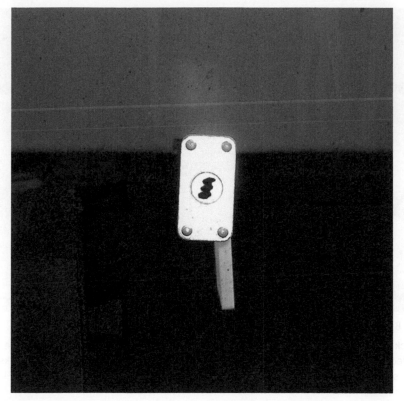

FIGURE 6.27

The lightning bolt keyway was an immediate sign. My smallest warded pick worked instantly to open it, giving me direct access to the electrical controls within.

Somewhat separate from all of this is the matter of *much* older locks which have been designated as "warded" locks by some historians. Certain locks that feature the classic "key hole" style aperture on the front make use of "warding" in a number of ways to improve their security, either by affecting which keys can be inserted or which keys can turn inside of the lock. While it is not wrong to call these "warded" locks, I tend to refer to them as *lever locks* (or, perhaps more properly, as "warded lever locks") because that is truly the mechanism by which these devices are either opened or shut. Warding is playing a role in how their keys *interact* with the levers contained inside these locks... but they are not *exclusively* operating by warded mechanisms alone.

Perhaps a future edition of this book may be able to afford the space and time to delve further into these styles of locks... but for now they remain beyond our scope. If you ever encounter a 19th-century warded lever lock on a penetration test, I'd love to hear about it!

FIGURE 6.28

This lock (found on an outdoor shed, which is not surprising) uses a warded key that is entirely one-sided. This is not as typical by modern standards, and although current warded picks can open this lock, it is slightly more awkward to use them.

SUMMARY

While warded locks can hardly be considered high-security devices, they remain popular and are still sold today due to their ease of manufacture, low cost, and capability to withstand harsh environmental conditions.

It is often trivial to modify the keys from one warded lock in order to make them function in many, many other warded locks. A key modified by removing material until only the "bare bones" remain is known as a *skeleton key*. Skeleton keys (and their counterpart, warded picks) work by touching *only* the internal components of a lock that release the shackle, bypassing everything else.

Although they offer little security, warded locks are often encountered on a day-to-day basis, particularly in outdoor locations. If you have warded picks or skeleton keys with you on a penetration testing job, you frequently can employ them to access telecommunications equipment, roofs and basements, or just to get past perimeter fencing.

Whatever you do, I strongly recommend against relying on warded locks for your own security. Plenty of alternate designs of locks exist that offer resistance to harsh conditions but which do not sacrifice robustness and protection in the process. The rotating-disk products from the Abloy company are one example. Locks featuring magnets such as those sold by Miwa and EVVA are also terrific alternatives. They do cost significantly more, but they cannot be compromised simply by someone with a key that they fashioned with a hand file or rotary tool in under a minute.

SmartKey Attacks

INTRODUCTION

In the middle of the ought years, while the public was gripped by headlines of Hurricane Katrina, escalating conflict in Iraq, North Korea's nuclear aims, and George W. Bush beginning his second term as President of the United States, another topic of concern percolated through the media, sending shivers of unease through the populace. Various reporters and columnists began talking about "bump keys" and "bumping locks" in stories that captivated and frightened many people. I was interviewed more than once on this topic, appearing on TV while a news anchor sat in my kitchen as she learned how to use a bump key.

I have treated bumping attacks both in this book and in my previous work. They are relatively clear-cut and can be effectively employed against many vulnerable locks. Of course, there are a number of locks that are immune to this attack, but by 2007 the "threat" of bump keys became widely-feared enough that manufacturers saw an opening in the market... anyone who could advertise a truly "bump-proof" lock would be able to capitalize on the public's apprehension and see a boost in sales.

One of the first products to be prominently advertised as "bump-proof" was an interesting offering from Kwikset (a division of Black & Decker and one of the most recognized names in locks in the United States). Known as their "Smart Series" line and designed to be instantly re-keyable by the user (as opposed to by a locksmith, who normally must remove and partially disassemble a lock to change its bitting combination), these new locks, touted under the name "SmartKey," grabbed people's attention. There was talk among landlords and vacation property owners of how convenient they were. There was chatter on locksport message boards about how difficult they were to pick. And there were plenty of security professionals discussing the fact that these locks truly were immune to bumping.

Soon enough, however, news began to emerge of vulnerabilities with these products. A company called Major Manufacturing produced a large tool (little more than a solid steel key mounted to a rod and handle) which could be used to smash the lock open, exploiting some of the weak metals used in the construction of early versions of the SmartKey. Of course, a destructive entry attack is not covert... but soon news also arose about this lock's susceptibility to a decoding attack.

Noted security researcher and champion locksport competitor Shane Lawson performed a detailed analysis of the Kwikset SmartKey system and presented his research at the ShmooCon and NotACon conferences in February and April of 2009, respectively. Video of this presentation is available at http://vimeo. com/4151972. Shane demonstrated to the assembled crowds that it was possible—using entirely home-made tools which cost very little to produce—to decode the bitting combination of a SmartKey lock. Audiences were awed over the fact that this attack is performed entirely from the exterior of the lock, that it takes very little time, and that it leaves virtually no forensic traces. This chapter tells the story of that attack.

THE KWIKSET SMARTKEY SYSTEM

You may have already observed a lock from Kwikset's SmartSeries line of products. If you have ever seen a doorknob or deadbolt that prominently featured a small slot in the front face of the plug, to the left (if the lock is mounted in the "pins up" configuration which is conventional for the North American market) of the keyway as can be seen in Figure 7.1, then you have encountered a Kwikset SmartKey lock.

In spite of its weaknesses, the SmartKey system is something of a marvel. It adequately fulfills the market demands for which it was conceived—it provides picking resistance, guarantees bumping immunity, and offers the user greater management and servicing control—by means of some very unique engineering. Figures 7.2 through 7.5 offer an inside look at how the mechanisms in this lock operate.

FIGURE 7.1

All Kwikset SmartKey locks feature a small rectangular slot on the face of the plug, to the left of the keyway, as seen here.

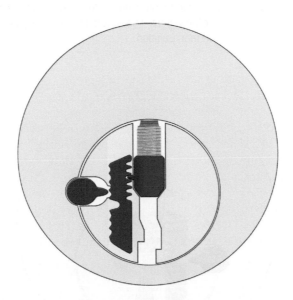

FIGURE 7.2

The SmartKey system boasts an interesting design. Although it is possible to view "pins" if you peer down into the keyway, this lock is technically a *wafer* lock. When a key is inserted, it interacts with *guide pins* that ride along the blade, carrying the wafers with them.

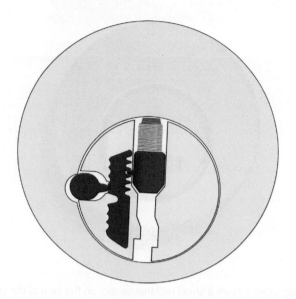

FIGURE 7.3

The plug of a SmartKey lock is prevented from turning by means of a sidebar. If turning pressure is applied to the plug (say, in an attempt to manipulate the lock) this will force the sidebar inward… but it will merely encounter the wafers. The wafers feature many *false notches* which interfere with attempts at picking and manipulation.

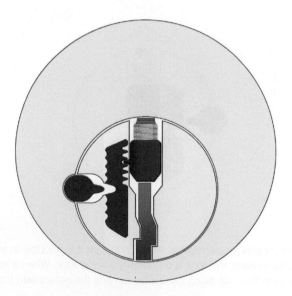

FIGURE 7.4

When the correct key is inserted into a SmartKey-style lock, the guide pins and wafers are raised to such a height that the sidebar is free to move completely into the plug.

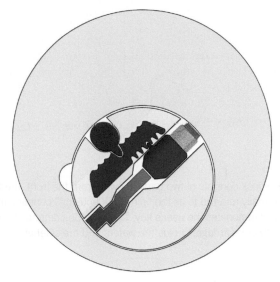

FIGURE 7.5

If the wafers are raised to the proper height and the side bar drops in, the plug can turn and the lock can open.

A full description of how the "user-re-keyable" feature of the Kwikset SmartKey system functions is a bit beyond the scope of what we will discuss here, but I will explain that a small, included tool can be employed in order to disengage the wafers and the guide pins from one another. The user is then free to remove the current working key, insert a new key, and re-engage the wafer and guide pin components. Thus, with no disassembly, the lock can easily be made to operate with a different key.

If you look closely at the wafers shown in the aforementioned figures (which appear in brown in those diagrams) you will see that they have a series of teeth down the *right* side. Unlike the notches on the left side, these are not related to the sidebar. These teeth are the various points at which the guide pin is able to engage with the wafer in order to open the lock at various bitting depths.

Unfortunately, the very components which power the lock's re-keyable functionality also weaken its overall security. The teeth on the right side of the wafers leak information, and due to how the lock functions these teeth are directly accessible through the keyway. This latest point may not be entirely clear in the diagrams shown up to this point, so please allow me to explain further. Figure 7.6 tries to convey a rather peculiar aspect of these locks… the plug is not actually one solid, round piece; rather, it consists of two halves. (The fact that these halves are separate is a critical component of how the re-keying functionality works, since they allow the wafers and the guide pins to disengage from one another.) Because the component on the right side is larger, that alone is sometimes referred to as the "plug" while the component on the left I have occasionally

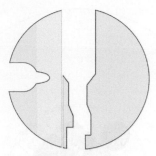

FIGURE 7.6

The plug of a SmartKey lock consists of two parts. Viewed from the front, the larger right-side component, often informally referred to as the "pin stack housing" contains the guide pins and their springs; it also accommodates the user's key. The left-side component, which my associates and I typically call the "wafer carriage," holds the wafers and the sidebar.

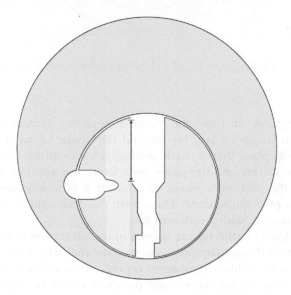

FIGURE 7.7

This diagram shows the plug and housing of a SmartKey lock without any pins, wafers, and so forth. While it may not be obvious from a front-perspective diagram like this, the region indicated by the purple arrow is wide open in each pin position inside the plug. This open space exists because the guide pins and wafers must interface with one another.

heard described with terms such as "wafer carriage" or "wafer pack." Personally, I feel the whole affair—both pieces put together—would be most appropriately thought of as the plug, and I routinely refer to the right-side component as the "pin stack housing" or "pin array side" or simply "the keyway and pins."

Because the guide pins contained in the right-side portion of the plug must interface with the wafers housed on the left, there are "windows" of open space where these two pieces meet. Figure 7.7 shows the SmartKey lock without any wafers, pins, springs, or sidebar. The portion of the plug marked by the long purple arrow is not solid. In this span, both the wafer carriage and the pin stack housing are machined with a series of open slots. Again, these slots are necessary so that the small "lip" on the edge of each guide pin can reach through and engage with its associated wafer. Figure 7.8 is a photograph showing only the right half of the plug (the pin stack housing) removed from a SmartKey lock; the large open slots in each bitting position can be clearly seen here, and the guide pins (as well as a key which is inserted into the plug at that moment) are visible through these open holes.

FIGURE 7.8

This is a pin stack housing that has been removed from a SmartKey lock. (In this photograph, the guide pins have been digitally colorized with a red hue in order to correlate with the other diagrams in this chapter. In reality, the guide pins have a dull gray luster.) In this image you can clearly see the slots which offer an exposed window directly into the keyway. Not only are the guide pins visible through these apertures, but even portions of the blade of a key can be seen (the brass-colored metal showing through beneath the artificial red of the guide pins)... it is this open design that causes the wafers to have direct exposure into the keyway. *(Photo courtesy of datagram.)*

DECODING SMARTKEY LOCKS

It was in late 2008 that Shane Lawson investigated ways of turning the "windowed" feature of this lock into an attack vector. It did not take him long to develop a unique exploit tool, made entirely out of a blank Kwikset key and simple materials. Upon disassembling and inspecting the lock, Lawson immediately realized that if a blank key were to be inserted into any Kwikset SmartSeries product, this would raise the wafers to such a height that their bitting teeth (the teeth on the right side of the wafers which interact with the guide pins) would be exposed through the open slots in each pin position (see Figures 7.9 and 7.10).

The tool which Shane Lawson created in order to exploit Kwikset SmartSeries products does not allow an attacker to immediately *open* the lock; rather, it is used to perform a *decoding* attack. If successful, the attacker will know the positions of all wafers relative to the guide pins and they will have the bitting code for the lock, which can then be used to produce a working key. While it is not an instant-entry technique, the SmartKey Decoder tool provides a trivial means of gaining consistent and repeated entry in a way that is virtually impossible to detect after-the-fact.

Figure 7.11 shows the simple elegance of the Kwikset SmartKey Decoder. It is a blank key with a long slot milled into the blade. Into this slot is inserted a long needle with a miniscule piece of metal on the tip, informally called a "pennant" by the tool's creator.[1] Readers who understood the previous diagrams can likely already envision how this specialized key is used. As can be seen in

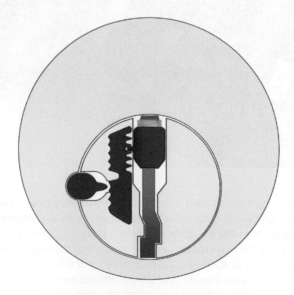

FIGURE 7.9

If a blank key is inserted into a SmartSeries lock, the guide pins (and, in turn, the wafers next to them) will all be raised up considerably.

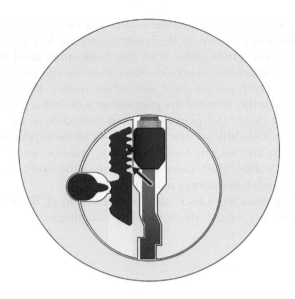

FIGURE 7.10

When a blank key is lifting the wafers up to a considerable height, these *unused bitting teeth* are exposed to the keyway.

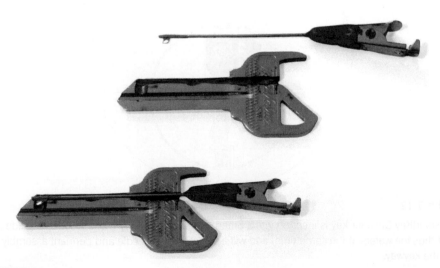

FIGURE 7.11

Shane Lawson's SmartKey Decoder tool is fashioned from a blank key. The blade of the key is milled with a long groove capable of accommodating a feeler element. The feeler is constructed from a long needle, equipped on one end with a handle and on the other end with a small metal pennant.

Figures 7.12 through 7.14, the groove which has been cut into the key blade allows the needle and pennant to be inserted into the keyway while the blank key itself is lifting the guide pins. With the guide pins (and thus the wafers) lifted up, the user rotates the needle in order to move the pennant around in an arc, feeling for the teeth on the right side of the wafer. By counting the teeth, an attacker can instantly discover the position at which the guide pin and wafer are currently interlocked. The pennant is then retired back into its groove, and the key is pulled out slightly so that the process can be repeated at the next pin position, and so on and so on. After a brief explanation and minimal training, it is our experience that most users are able to effectively decode a Kwikset SmartKey lock in under 10 minutes using this tool.

After the bitting code for a lock has been determined, it can then be used to produce a working key on a code-cutting key machine.

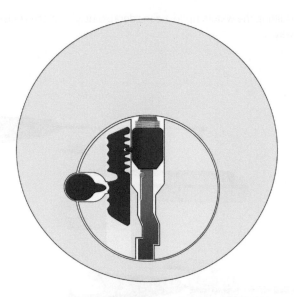

FIGURE 7.12

If a SmartKey Decoder key is inserted into a SmartSeries lock, the key blade will lift the guide pins (and thus the wafers at the same time) and will also deliver the needle and pennant assembly into the keyway.

---

[1] I should point out that Lawson's goal was to design the cheapest and simplest possible tool on purpose as a way to make a point about the perils of over-engineering.

FIGURE 7.13

In order to operate the SmartKey Decoder, the user simply rotates the handle when the pennant has been aligned at the correct position within the keyway. Often, small tick marks are added to the key blade so that the user can properly ease the key back out in order to interact with wafers at each pin position.

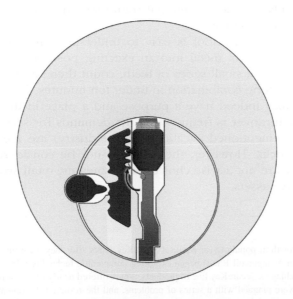

FIGURE 7.14

Inside the lock, the small metal pennant on the tip of the feeler will brush across the teeth on the right side of the wafers. It is not particularly difficult to feel for the unused teeth that are exposed beneath the lip on each guide pin. By counting these unused teeth, the user of this tool is able to discern the point at which the wafers and the guide pins are interlocked... this data, in turn, can be used to decode the bitting of whatever key is currently operating the lock.

TIP

A working key could also be fabricated by hand-filing with the aid of calipers, a depth key, or the notches on a key decoder card like the one shown earlier in Figure 1.67.

SUMMARY

The SmartSeries products from Kwikset were innovative and they are rather unique offerings in the world of physical security hardware. Technically, they should be thought of as *wafer locks* since it is the wafer mechanism which interacts with the sidebar and ultimately holds the lock shut or allows the plug to turn. Yes, these locks do feature "pins" in a manner of speaking, but they are not the primary drivers of the lock's functionality. The SmartKey system offers users fairly robust protection against casual lockpicking and eliminates the risk from bumping while simultaneously affording the user a means of quickly and easily changing what key may be used in a given door.

While features like this have made the lock very attractive to landlords and rental agencies, businesses and institutions requiring high security protection should not rely on hardware such as this. Researchers in the physical security community have exposed critical flaws in this technology which may allow attackers to quickly decode the internal configuration of a SmartKey lock, leaving little trace of their activities.

The SmartKey Decoder tool is easy to understand and simple to use. By inserting a small piece of metal into an exacting position within the keyway, one can brush across a small series of teeth, count them, and discern the lock's current working bitting combination in under ten minutes.

These locks may indeed have a purpose and a place in the market... situations where key turnover is frequent but the demands for security are minimal (as with the aforementioned vacation rental industry) are ideal situations for user-re-keyable locks. However, these should not be considered high-security devices and they are not a wise choice for businesses, retail spaces, or the protection of sensitive assets.

NOTE

Due to the rapid growth in popularity of Kwikset SmartKey locks after they were introduced, the Schlage company (a division of Ingersoll Rand) began exploring comparable technology. In 2009 the market saw the emergence of Schlage's SecureKey line of products, which offered nearly identical functionality.

These devices were plagued with a series of problems, and the resultant discontent among locksmiths (along with an infringement lawsuit from Kwikset) led Schlage to discontinue the SecureKey line at the end of 2011. I have not had the opportunity to examine these locks in great depth and therefore do not know at this time if a similar type of decoding attack would be possible against them. Because of this hardware's retirement from the marketplace, I have not made such research a priority, but if I do explore and learn about the SecureKey system I will be sure to include my findings in an updated version of this book in the future.

Don't Let Your Keys Talk to Strangers

8

CHAPTER OUTLINE

INTRODUCTION

In the 1999 film *The Thomas Crown Affair* there is a segment during which Catherine Banning, a sassy investigator played by Rene Russo, and her team of security professionals wish to secretly enter the home of a billionaire suspected of art theft. Their target is the eponymous Thomas Crown (played by Pierce Brosnan). During the course of an evening out with this gentleman, Banning concocts a ruse to borrow his overcoat, using this as an opportunity to covertly pass Crown's house keys to one of her associates. What follows is a frenzied race on the part of Banning's team as they rush to a locksmith shop where copies of all the keys can be made. They then must dash back to the couple and slip the keys back into the jacket pocket before Crown reclaims his coat at the end of the evening. All this makes for rather good cinema, but nothing quite so involved is ever truly necessary in the field.

The simple fact is that, if someone can gain control of a key for *just a few minutes* it will likely be possible for them to compromise that key entirely. We saw examples of cast-and-mold techniques in Chapter 2, but even more possibilities exist for an attacker to discern the bitting data of your keys in order to make copies elsewhere.

KEY DECODING

Way back in Chapter 1 I introduced you to the locksmithing tool known as a *key decoder card*. Consisting simply of a series of graduated slots, it is used to quickly and effectively measure the depths of every cut on the blade of typical keys (see Figure 8.1).

However, a key decoder card is somewhat obvious to any individuals who have been educated about locksmithing or other aspects of physical security. If you are attempting to exfiltrate key bitting data from a facility that tightly restricts what items are permissible through its doors, you may have better luck with *depth keys*.

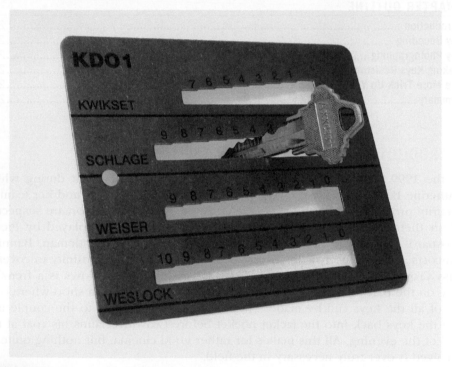

FIGURE 8.1

A key decoder card is a very effective means of measuring bitting cuts on the blade of a key.
(Photo courtesy of Patrick Thomas.)

Depth keys

Depth keys are nothing more than conventional keys that have been cut in a predictable pattern on a code-cutting key machine. Usually produced with a simple "staircase" pattern, a depth key might have a bitting code of 1-2-3-4-5-6 or 1-3-5-7-9.

If you happen across an unattended key and you know that it opens a particularly useful lock or door, a depth key can be held directly next to this target key in order to compare the bitting cuts and decode the depth values. Figure 8.2 shows a sampling of depth keys and Figure 8.3 depicts how they are used.

Because of the inherent limitations in the creation of depth keys (the fact that the number of different depths usually exceeds the number of available bitting positions available on the key) it is sometimes helpful to get a little creative. While it was not exactly within specification for the machine, I was able to make TOOOL's UltraCode key machine produce a key with a bitting of 1-2-3-4-5-6-7-8-9 using a blank from an EasyEntrie system. It might look a bit funny (see Figure 8.4) but no one has actually ever questioned why I have this key or refused me entrance to a secure building when I have been carrying it. I have used it to decode Schlage keys in the field, including at least one that turned out to be the top master key for a five-star hotel.

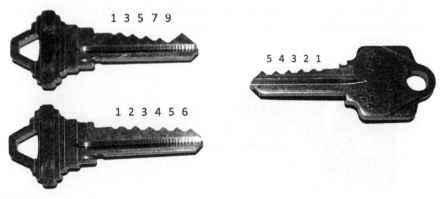

FIGURE 8.2

Left: Two Schlage SC4 depth keys. Right: An Arrow AR1 depth key. In many instances, manufacturers will have more bitting depths than there are positions on a typical key. For example, Schlage keys have nine distinct possible bitting depths but no Schlage key has more than six pin positions; there is no feasible way to incorporate them all on a single depth key. Hence, the two distinct Schlage keys... one is a simple progression from 1 through 6; the other shows only odd-numbered cut depths but manages to reach a depth of 9 in this fashion.

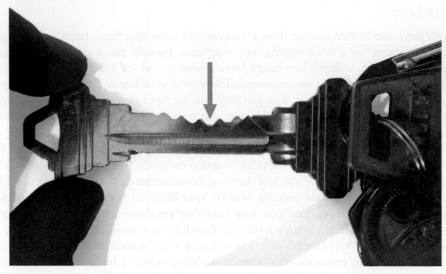

FIGURE 8.3

The depth key seen in the upper-left of Figure 8.2 is being used here to measure bitting cuts on a Schlage key found in the field. A particularly deep cut on the target key appears deeper than a 5-cut, but it is clearly not as deep as a 7-cut on the depth key. Thus, we know that the key being measured must have a bitting value of 6 in that position.

FIGURE 8.4

This is my "all nine bitting cut values on a single key" solution, created using an Easy Entrie blank rholex.

KEY PHOTOGRAPHING

Even if you are unable to directly *handle* a target key, often it is still quite possible to decode the cuts visually. The evolution of consumer electronics technology has produced cameras and video recording equipment that is increasingly compact. Modern smart phones are ideal for surreptitious imaging of keys and other valuable intelligence as you walk through a facility.

FIGURE 8.5

These keys were left on a table in a high-security development and engineering lab. All it took was a moment with my BlackBerry to photograph them while I pretended to be checking email. A helpful trick that you can do (especially if a key is for a brand of lock that you don't often encounter) is to toss a coin on the desk before you take a picture. It can serve as a standard size guide later on as you analyze the photograph.

Figure 8.5 shows keys found lying on a desk in an engineering lab. Even though this image was captured simply with the camera on my BlackBerry, the keys were leaking more than enough information for us to attempt producing copies at a later time. You would be astonished at how far away it is possible to be from keys and still successfully execute this attack. Students at the Jacobs School of Engineering at the University of California, San Diego, experimented with telephoto lenses and the use of some computer-aided modeling to mathematically assist them in successfully determining the bitting of keys from nearly 200 feet away. You can easily Google for additional accounts of their *Sneakey* system or their academic paper, "Reconsidering Physical Key Secrecy: Teleduplication via Optical Decoding." If that isn't an inspiration for you to keep your keys safely tucked in your pocket, then I don't know what is (see Figure 8.6).

Of course perhaps the easiest way that your keys may reveal crucial data is through stamped bitting codes. Look at your keys. How many of them have numbers on the bow? Often, these digits can provide very useful data to an

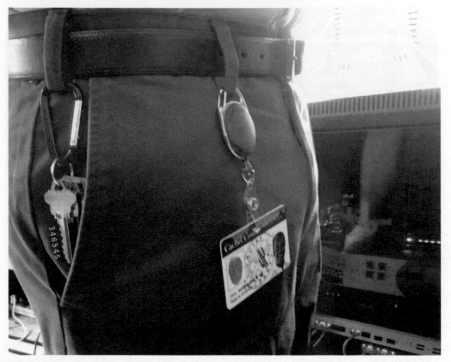

FIGURE 8.6

This individual carelessly left his keys exposed by hanging them from his belt. Documenting them (at least, the ones which were showing) was not difficult. I have superimposed the bitting combination for the left-most Schlage key onto this image. *Also captured was this man's security badge which can be useful if you are attempting to duplicate someone's credentials in order to appear less suspicious while walking around a target facility.*

attacker. Figure 8.7 shows two keys that are marked with their direct bitting code. Occasionally (particularly with higher-security locks) the numbers stamped onto a key are a *blind code* which is only useful if one has access to a lookup table or reference book... still, I often prefer to have keys that never bear markings of this sort.

FIGURE 8.7

These two keys both have codes stamped on their bows. On the left we see a Yale key with bitting 3-4-6-5-4-5. On the right the silver key's bitting is 1-1-4-4-6. Looking at the blades of these keys it is quite clear that these are direct bitting codes. If these keys protect anything even slightly valuable, the owners would do well to have them duplicated and then *not* have any numbers stamped on the new copies.

MAKING KEYS RESISTANT TO DECODING

If you wish to prevent an assailant from easily decoding your keys, there are steps that you can take. The simplest tactic is, of course, to simply maintain as much as control over your keys as possible. Carry them in your pocket and do not loan them or leave them lying about.

However, if you desire an extra degree of protection against visual decoding, you might opt to have a locksmith cut your keys in a non-standard way.

Many people are familiar with the typical process that a key machine will usually use: moving the high-speed wheel into each position in turn, cutting down to the requisite depth, retracting the wheel, and moving on. This tends to produce a key with many sharp points in between each bitting position.

In Chapter 1 of my first book, *Practical Lock Picking*, I demonstrated to readers that these triangular points are not actually necessary for operation of most pin tumbler locks. A key produced without them would be perfectly adequate (see Figure 8.8). Indeed, a good number of code-cutting key machines are able to produce results like this automatically. This is done by setting the machine for *flat mode* cutting. Not only will this allow a key to be inserted and

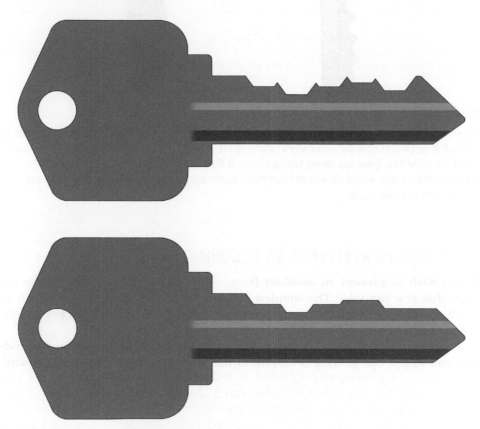

FIGURE 8.8

Top: A conventional key, produced in *standard* mode, will feature points of metal rising up in between each bitting cut. Bottom: A key produced in *flat mode* will have a different appearance, with no points in between each bitting position.

removed from a lock more smoothly, reducing wear and tear on the pins, but it will also eliminate much of the possibility of the key making holes in the fabric of your pockets.

Some key machines offer even fancier ways of producing keys, however. Ilco's UltraCode line of devices (one of which appeared in Figure 1.47 in Chapter 1) are capable of operating in *laser mode* when cutting keys. The resultant keys, as you can see in Figure 8.9, have a very atypical look. Believe it or not, both of those pictured keys have the exact same bitting code. They both operate the same lock. However, one is trivial to decode (either visually or with the aid of a depth card, etc.) while the other would offer a considerable challenge, particularly to someone working only from a photograph.

NOTE

Contrary to what some people may think, no laser beam is employed in the cutting of any key produced in *laser mode* such as the one seen in Figure 8.9. Movies and TV shows about law enforcement or criminal heists will occasionally make passing reference to "laser cut keys" or "laser encoded keys" and the like. This is mostly just dramatic mock jargon.

While it would be entirely possible to use laser to cut metals—indeed, rapid prototyping labs and high-tech fabrication shops use lasers along with other interesting methods such as water jetting or CNC milling or photochemical etching in order to produce metal components—this is not economically practical for something like the cutting of keys.

FIGURE 8.9

These two keys actually have the exact same bitting values. The top key was produced using standard cutting methods; the bottom key was produced on an Ilco UltraCode machine operating in laser mode.

ONE MORE TRICK UP YOUR SLEEVE

Let's say that you are in a building that is *very* tightly-controlled. You cannot carry your pick tools. You cannot have your mobile phone or any type of camera with you. You cannot even risk trying to slip a key decoder card into your wallet. Is there anything that you might do should you happen across an unsecured key? You wouldn't want to risk stealing it outright… a facility that prohibits photography and has metal detectors at the doors is likely to notice a missing key.

While it is not the most reliable method of recording the bitting data from a key, you can always try simply rolling up your sleeve and pressing the metal directly into your forearm for 30 seconds or more (see Figure 8.10). It won't make the most ideal copy, but you'd be surprised how long such an imprint will remain on your arm. It should be clearly legible and able to be photographed or measured using calipers for the next five to fifteen minutes (see Figure 8.11).

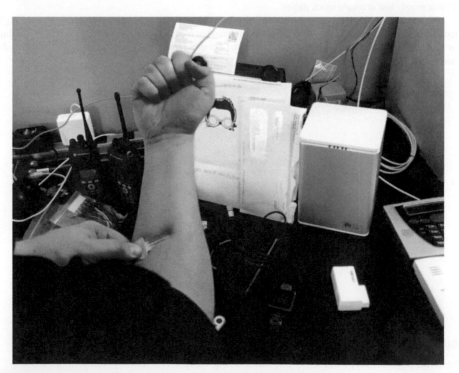

FIGURE 8.10

Pressing a key directly into your arm for a half-minute or more will leave a considerable imprint. Even details like sidebar bittings tend to make an impression and stick with you for a while.

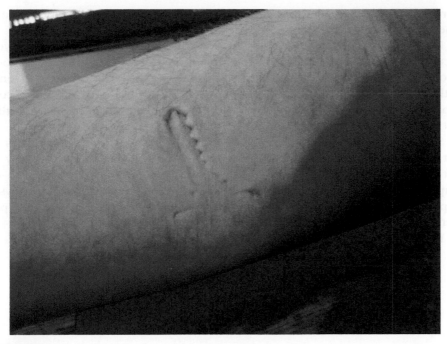

FIGURE 8.11

It wouldn't be a suitable negative for a cast-and-mold attack, but this key-shaped mark might remain long enough for you to exit a facility and take more exacting measurements outside if you have a caliper or other tools in your vehicle.

SUMMARY

While some of the tactics described in this chapter might seem far-fetched, I hope they illustrate the point that your keys are capable of leaking incredibly revealing information unless you keep them protected. Be on guard against attacks such as manual decoding, photographic decoding, and the like by simply being vigilant about how you carry your keys when you need them and where you store keys when you are not using them.

Keys are remarkable objects, given how much access a person can potentially gain by compromising or exploiting them. In the end, no one key should ever be able to grant *anybody*, even an authorized user, total access to an entire facility or campus. Yes, top master keys exist in many large systems and highly valuable keys are part of even small infrastructures… but *locks and keys themselves* should never be your only line of defense.

Design your security in layers. Plan for the occasional key being lost or perhaps even compromised. How effectively would your security withstand intrusion if that were to happen? Good security is based on the principle of "the three R's"... Resist, Recognize, Recover.

Not only should your locks, access controls, alarms, and the rest of your security system simply *resist* entry to unauthorized persons, but they should also have the capability to *recognize* when someone is attempting to enter without proper privileges. If part of your security posture is weakened or compromised, you should still have the ability to *recover* in such a way that all is not lost.

Simple metal keys alone cannot provide this level of protection. Keys do not know who is holding them. They do not know what time it is. They do not know if they are being used by a CEO during the workday or by an ex-employee in the middle of the night. Having good locks with robust keys is important, but this mustn't be your only focus when you plan how to best protect yourself and your assets from others.

Best wishes, and stay safe out there!

Index

Note: Page numbers followed by "f" refer to figures

Printed and bound by CPI Group (UK) Ltd, Croydon, CR0 4YY
03/11/2024
03040320-0006

Printed and bound by CPI Group (UK) Ltd, Croydon, CR0 4YY

03/10/2024

01040325-0006